WRATH and GLORY

Sharlene—

May God bless your
study of Revelation

Maranatha!

Dave Reagan

6/2002

WRATH and GLORY

UNVEILING THE MAJESTIC BOOK OF REVELATION

Dr. David R. Reagan

New Leaf Press

First printing: August 2001

ISBN: 0-89221-511-9
Library of Congress Catalog Number: 01-91123

Cover painting by Phelan Douglas Hicks

All Scripture quotations in this book, unless otherwise noted,
are taken from the New American Standard Bible © 1995 by
the Lockman Foundation. Used by permission.

Printed in the United States of America

Please visit our website for other great titles:
www.newleafpress.net

For information regarding publicity for author
interviews contact Dianna Fletcher at (870) 438-5288.

Men will go into caves of the rocks,
And into holes of the ground Before the
terror of the LORD And the splendor
of His majesty, When He arises to
make the earth tremble.

Isaiah 2:19

Dedicated to
my grandson, Jason Smith

He does not know who he is,
nor does he know who I am.
But one day soon, when Jesus returns,
his mind will be healed
and I will enjoy his fellowship forever.

The sufferings of this present time are not worthy
to be compared with the glory that is to be revealed to us.
Romans 8:18

Contents

List of Illustrations

Preface

Winston Churchill once said that Russia is "a riddle wrapped in a mystery inside an enigma." That's the way most Christians view the Book of Revelation. They shudder at the thought of reading or studying it. That is a shame because, as I hope to show in this book, it is a spiritual gem that can be understood and applied to our lives here and now. You don't have to be a rocket scientist nor do you have to be clairvoyant to understand it.

I want to express my appreciation to Mrs. H. Grant Hicks of Henryville, Indiana, for permission to use the incredible painting *Messhia* on the cover of this book. It was painted by her son, Phelan Douglas Hicks, when he was only 17 years old. Two years later he drowned in Lake Michigan while doing mission work in the Chicago inner city.

The Book of Revelation is full of vivid pictures like the one painted by Douglas Hicks. Those pictures have become a part of my soul, and their message has been a great blessing to me. I want to share that blessing with you. As you read this book, I pray that you will be drawn into a deeper relationship with Jesus. I pray, too, that your hope will be greatly enhanced as you come to a better understanding of the incredible promises that God has made about the future.

Understanding Revelation

T he Book of Revelation is a Chinese puzzle that no one can understand!" I must have heard those words a hundred times when I was growing up in the Church. Guess what? I wrote the book off as a lost cause and ignored it for 30 years. Why waste time trying to decipher a mysterious book that even biblical scholars could not understand?

For the past 20 years I have been teaching Bible prophecy all across America and around the world. As I have talked with Christians from all denominations, I have discovered that most are ignorant of the Book of Revelation, and many are downright afraid of it.

The Significance of Revelation

This is the state of affairs for the Church as a whole as well as for individual Christians. It's like reading a great novel, but never reading the last chapter to see how the story comes out. Reading and understanding the Book of Revelation is vitally important to Christendom because it tells us that *we are going to win in the end!* It is a book of victory that is designed to encourage Christians as they try to cope with and overcome this pagan world.

Studying the Book of Revelation today, at the beginning of the 21st century, is particularly important because Christians are faced with two great challenges — the decay of society and growing apostasy in the Church.[1] As we face these grim realities, we need the encouragement that is contained in the Book of Revelation.

There is another reason we should be focusing on the Book of Revelation at the beginning of the 21st century. The signs of the times clearly indicate that we are living in the last days — that Jesus is at the very gates of heaven waiting for His Father's command to return. The state of Israel has been re-established. The Jews are back in Jerusalem. Europe has united. And modern technology has given meaning to numerous prophecies that we never understood before.

One hundred years ago there were no signs at all which indicated the Lord's soon return. The first sign appeared in 1917 when the Balfour Declaration was issued by the British government, promising that Palestine would be turned into a homeland for the Jews. Today, there are so many signs pointing to the Lord's soon return that one would have to be spiritually blind not to discern them. I am no longer looking for signs; I am listening for sounds — for the blast of a trumpet and the shout of an angel: "The Bridegroom comes!"

Glory or Wrath?

Jesus is returning soon, and that fact makes the Book of Revelation relevant to our lives. The book begins and ends with the promise that Jesus will return. It is the theme of the book. In Revelation 1:7 we are told, "Behold he is coming with the clouds, and every eye will see Him, even those who pierced Him." The book ends with Jesus himself making the same proclamation: "Behold, I am coming quickly, and My reward is with Me, to render to every man according to what he has done." (Rev. 22:12)

The return of Jesus will be the climactic event of history. For some, it will be the most glorious day of their lives, for Jesus will come as their glory — as their "blessed hope" (Titus

2:13). For others, His return will be a terrifying experience, for He will come as their holy terror, pouring out the wrath of God upon all those who have rejected God's gift of love, grace, and mercy (Rev. 19:11).

The Bible says that every person on the face of this earth is under either the wrath of God or His grace: "He who believes in the Son has eternal life; but he who does not obey the Son shall not see life, but the wrath of God abides on him" (John 3:36). It is glory to be under the grace of God. It is terror to be under His wrath.

The return of Jesus will mean glory or wrath for each of us. It will mean both for Jesus. When He returns to this earth, He will come in wrath to judge and make war against the enemies of God (Rev. 19:11). But the wrath will be followed by glory as He is crowned the King of kings and Lord of lords and begins His majestic reign from Mount Zion as the "Prince of Peace" (Isa. 9:6). He will manifest His glory before the nations (Isa. 24:21–23), and He will receive the honor and praise which He was denied when He came the first time (2 Thess. 1:10).

Wrath and glory — these two words sum up the meaning of the Lord's return for you and me and Him.

God in His unfathomable grace does not desire that any should perish, but that all should be brought to repentance and salvation (2 Pet. 3:9). God has therefore given us the magnificent Book of Revelation to warn us of His wrath and to call us to His glory. When we stand before Him, we will have no excuses. He has spelled it all out for us in advance and in detail in the Book of Revelation.

The Neglect of Prophecy

Let's begin our consideration of Revelation by looking at two verses from 2 Timothy 3 — verses 16 and 17. Paul wrote these words to a young preacher: "All Scripture is inspired by God and profitable for teaching, for reproof, for correction, for training in righteousness; so that the man of God may be adequate, equipped for every good work."

These are verses that most Christians know very well. You may know them by heart because you've memorized them, or you may have them almost memorized because you've heard them so many times. You're probably wondering why in the world someone would begin a study of the Book of Revelation with these two verses.

Well, I'll tell you why. There is no portion of God's Word that has been more ignored by students of the Bible and by the Church in general than God's prophetic Word. This is incredible when you consider the fact that almost one-third of the Bible is prophetic in nature.

Let me give you an example of what I'm talking about. Most young men studying to be preachers today will go all the way through seminary and never take one course on Bible prophecy. They'll graduate and preach for years and never preach one sermon on Bible prophecy. They, in effect, ignore one-third of God's Holy Word.

That's unfortunate because Paul says by inspiration of the Holy Spirit that *all* Scripture — not just the New Testament, not just the history books of the Old Testament, but *all* Scripture — is inspired by God. That includes Bible prophecy. When Paul said that "all Scripture is profitable for teaching, for reproof, for correction, for training in righteousness; so that the man of God might be adequate, equipped for every good work," he meant that statement to include Bible prophecy.

All of God's Word is practical, down to earth, and is necessary if we are to be shaped by the Holy Spirit into the image of Jesus. We need all of God's Word, and that includes God's prophetic Word, and that includes the Book of Revelation.

A Personal Experience

I guess I grew up in a pretty typical church. I was raised in a church that emphasized the New Testament and ignored Bible prophecy. I went to church faithfully every time the door was open. I was there Sunday morning, Sunday night, Wednesday night, and during vacation Bible school. Yet, after 30 years of going to church, I knew absolutely nothing about Bible prophecy because we almost totally ignored it.

Any time we got into a study of prophecy, we just ran over it very quickly and tried to get through with it as soon as we possibly could. The result was that after 30 years of going to church, I was so ignorant of Bible prophecy that if you had asked me what the Rapture was, I probably would have said, "It's a sensation you feel when your girlfriend kisses you!" In like manner, I would probably have identified Gog and Magog as a comedy team. The Antichrist to me was a "denominational preacher," because we thought we were non-denominational, and we thought we were the only true church.

We just simply ignored God's prophetic word. The tragic consequence is that our spiritual growth was stunted. Our sanctification — that is, our development into the image of Jesus — was delayed because the spirit of Man was designed to feed upon the Word of God — not just the New Testament, not just the Old Testament, but *all* of God's Word.

The Major Barrier to Revelation

The preachers that I grew up under generally took the position that the Book of Revelation was impossible to understand. I think about the only time we studied the book was when a minister got a little carried away and would make a rash commitment by saying, "I tell you what we're going to do. We're going to start with the Book of Matthew, and we're going to go all the way through the New Testament and study every book." Three years later when he reached the Book of Revelation, he would regret that he ever made the promise. But he had made it, and, therefore, he felt like he was obligated to keep it.

So, he would get up before the congregation and say something like this: "Well, folks, I made the vow we'd go all the way through the New Testament. We've reached the Book of Revelation. I'll tell you right now, nobody can understand it. Nobody ever has. Nobody ever will. It's a Chinese puzzle."

I can't begin to tell you how many times I've heard that.

"Yes, it's a Chinese puzzle," the minister would emphasize. "So I'll tell you what we'll do. We'll study it the next few Wednesday nights and try to get through it as quickly as we can."

Guess what happened? The attendance fell off drastically as the preacher got up and tried to muddle his way through this book that he considered a puzzle. He didn't understand it. How in the world he thought he could teach it to anybody, I don't know.

The effect was to create a psychological barrier in my mind. I have since discovered that this mental barrier against the book exists in the thinking of most professing Christians, regardless of what church they grew up in.

A Book for Theologians or Fanatics?

In most churches, either the Book of Revelation has been ignored completely or people have been convinced that it is an enigma that nobody can understand unless maybe you have a Ph.D. in hermeneutics, whatever that is. Perhaps if you have that, or a vivid imagination, you might understand the book.

The general attitude in Christendom seems to be that the Book of Revelation is something for only two types of people. It's for the doctor of theology, who has degrees piled on top of degrees. It's for him to toy with in an attempt to decipher the deep and hidden spiritual meanings. Or it's for the fanatic to play with as he searches for the Antichrist under every rock.

So that is the problem that we have in Christendom regarding the Book of Revelation. We have a tremendous psychological barrier against reading and understanding this marvelous book.

Again, the tragic result is that most Christians have never read the book. And you know what? Satan really loves that.

Satanic Deceptions

Satan does not want anybody to read the Book of Revelation. You know why? Because the book tells how everything is going to come out in the end. Satan wants to keep you in suspense. Satan wants to keep you guessing. Satan wants to keep your eyes focused on the wicked world in which we live so that you will think evil is going to triumph. His hope is that you will give up hope and decide to cast your lot with wickedness.

Satan doesn't want anybody reading the Book of Revelation because the book states in no uncertain terms that Satan is going to be totally defeated and Jesus Christ is going to be completely victorious. The book reveals that the great cosmic battle of the universe that has gone on since the beginning of time is going to be won by God the Father, the Creator of the universe. And the book proclaims that those who have cast their lot with God by accepting His Son as Lord and Savior are going to reign with Him eternally.

A Message of Wrath and Glory

The Book of Revelation is a book of incredibly good news for those who are children of God. We are called by the Spirit to read it and believe it and draw hope from it. The book also contains some incredibly bad news because it presents a graphic picture of the pouring out of God's wrath upon those who have rejected Jesus.

Wrath and glory — that's the message of Revelation. The glory of Jesus' triumphant return and reign over all the world is something Christians can accept and even yearn for. But many find it difficult, if not impossible, to accept the concept of God pouring out His wrath. How can a God of love also be a God of wrath?

The Nature of God

One thing you have to understand is that God has two aspects to His nature. On one side He is full of grace and mercy and love — so much love that He sent His only begotten Son to die for the sins of the world even though we did not deserve it or merit it. But there is another aspect of God that is very rarely ever talked about, very rarely ever preached

about, and which most Christians know nothing about. The
other side of God's character is that He is perfectly just and
perfectly holy and perfectly righteous. And because He is perfectly just, holy, and righteous, He will not countenance sin.

As I said before, God deals with sin in one of two ways:
either with wrath or with grace (John 3:36). If you are under
grace, then Jesus will return as your blessed hope. But if you
are under the wrath of God, He will come as your holy terror.
Jesus is the love of God, and He is the wrath of God.

The Lamb and the Lion

Jesus came the first time as a suffering lamb to die for
the sins of mankind. Like a lamb, He walked meekly to the
Cross where He shed His blood to make it possible for us to
be reconciled to our Creator God. Through the sacrifice of
that gentle and pure Lamb, God provided forgiveness of our
sins (1 John 1:7).

But Jesus is not returning as a suffering lamb. No, He is
returning as a conquering lion (Jer. 25:30–31). He is going to
roar from the heavens, and He is going to pour out the wrath
of God upon those who have rejected the grace, the mercy,
and the love of God (Rev. 19:11–18).

A Balanced View of God

Again, I want to emphasize to you that God is going to
deal with sin. I want to emphasize this to you very strongly.
There is a passage in the Bible that graphically portrays this
truth. It's found in the Book of Nahum in the Old Testament.

Incidentally, Nahum is one of those Bible books that
most Christians have never read. Most probably couldn't even
find it. It's one of the so-called "Minor Prophets." I hate that
term because it makes the books sound unimportant. Nothing could be further from the truth. The Minor Prophets are
very important. The prophets who wrote them just happened
to be short-winded. They are "minor" only in the sense that
they are shorter in length than the "Major Prophets."

Now notice what Nahum says about the dual nature of

God and His determination to deal with sin. Nahum writes, "The Lord is good, a stronghold in the day of trouble, and He knows those who take refuge in Him" (Nah. 1:7). That's the image of God that most of us like to cherish. That's the way we like to think of God — a God full of love and kindness and grace and patience and mercy and strength — a God who will protect us in our day of trouble.

But notice verse 2: "A jealous and avenging God is the Lord; the Lord is avenging and wrathful." Now Nahum points us to the other aspect of God's character. And he continues, "The Lord takes vengeance on His adversaries, and He reserves wrath for His enemies. The Lord is slow to anger and great in power, and the Lord will by no means leave the guilty unpunished." Read it again — "The Lord is slow to anger and great in power, and the Lord will by no means leave the guilty unpunished" (Nah. 1:3). Those are ominous words.

A Perverted View of God

Satan has tried to create a false image of God as the Great Cosmic Teddy Bear, as the big, soft, warm, furry figure in the sky. Likewise, Satan has tried to create the impression that when we stand before the Lord to be judged, God is going to put His big, soft arm around us and pull us up close to Him and cuddle us and say, "Well, I know that you never accepted My Son as your Lord and Savior. But you lived a pretty good life, and you were certainly a lot better than the old reprobate down the street from you. And so, because of that, I'm going to overlook your sins and your rejection of my Son. Just come on into My kingdom and enjoy eternal life forevermore."

Let me tell you something. That is not the God of the Bible. God is going to deal with sin, and He deals with it with either grace or wrath. Jesus is the grace, and Jesus is the wrath. He came first in love. He is coming back in wrath. And He is going to pour out the wrath of God upon those who have rejected God's gift of love.

The Theme and the Focus

That brings us to the theme of Revelation. The book is a story about the second coming of Jesus Christ. From beginning to end it points us to the soon return of Jesus as our Lord and Savior. In fact, the theme of the book is mentioned in the very first chapter in verse 7. It says, "Behold, He is coming with the clouds, and every eye will see Him, even those who pierced Him; and all the tribes of the earth will mourn over Him. So it is to be. Amen." That's the theme of the whole book from beginning to end.

The focus of the book is upon what the Old Testament prophets called "the day of the Lord" (Joel 2:1). It is the time period that will begin with the Tribulation and climax with the millennial reign of Jesus. It includes the day of the Lord's second coming, which will occur at the end of the Tribulation.

Is it any wonder that Satan does not want us to read this book? That's why he has pretty well convinced the average Christian that the book is unintelligible, that the book cannot be understood, that it's simply a playground for intellectuals or fanatics, and that the average Christian should stay away from it. But once again, I want to remind you of the words of God in 2 Timothy 3:16–17: "All Scripture is inspired by God and profitable for teaching, for reproof, for correction, for training in righteousness; so that the man of God may be adequate, equipped for every good work." That is *all* Scripture, and that includes the Book of Revelation.

A Personal Victory

Let me tell you how I achieved my breakthrough in understanding the Book of Revelation. As I said before, for 30 years I thought it was a Chinese puzzle. For 30 years I avoided it like the plague. For 30 years I considered it to be a bunch of mumbo-jumbo.

And then one day in a moment of religious fervor, I made a vow to read the New Testament all the way through. When I got to the Book of Revelation, I thought, *I'm trapped. I made a vow, and now I've got to keep it.* I decided to read the book as fast as I could. But before I could start scanning it, I noticed something right off that I had never noticed before because the Holy Spirit of God brought it to my attention.

It was Revelation 1:3. Look what it says: "Blessed is he who reads and those who hear the words of the prophecy and heed the things which are written in it; for the time is near." Now, that really caught my eye. It jumped off the page at me. It witnessed to my spirit. "Blessed is he who reads the book or hears it read."

I'm a person who believes in the promises of God. I rejoice over the blessings He promises, and I want all the blessings He has to offer. I was excited to discover that the Book of Revelation is the only book in the Bible that starts off promising the reader a blessing for reading it.

You know what I did that night? I stopped reading, bowed my head, and claimed the blessing of Revelation 1:3 in advance in prayer. I said, "Lord God, the blessing that I want is the blessing of understanding this 'Chinese puzzle.' "

An Answered Prayer

I then read the book. You know what? I got some insights as I read it. I then got another version, and I prayed, "Lord, I claim Revelation 1:3 in prayer. And the blessing that I want, dear Lord, is the blessing of understanding." I read it all the way through. I got some more insights. I sought out another translation. I began to get excited because I was starting to understand what I was reading. I didn't understand everything, but some things were beginning to come together. Again, I claimed Revelation 1:3 in prayer. I said, "Lord God, give me the blessing. Give it to me in advance. I'm going to read it all the way through. You know I'm going to do it. Give me the blessing of understanding as I read."

Well, I've read the Book of Revelation hundreds of times since then, and every time I still pray, "Oh, Dear God, give me the blessing of Revelation 1:3. Help me to understand more this time than I have ever understood before." Every time God has been faithful to His promise. There are still things in the Book of Revelation I do not understand. There are probably some things that nobody understands. We're told in 1 Corinthians 13:12 that there are things in the Word of God that we can't understand fully because we are like a person looking into a dim mirror. But, says the passage, we will understand when we stand face to face with Jesus Christ.

Don't let that discourage you. Just keep in mind that there is a whole lot more in the Book of Revelation that you can understand than will ever be a mystery to you once you achieve the fundamental psychological breakthrough of believing that God wants you to understand it.

Keys to Understanding

The psychological breakthrough that I achieved is the first of several keys to understanding Revelation. There are some other keys that you need to keep in mind. I'm going to give you eight. I could give you more than that, but I'm just going to focus on the eight most important keys to understanding this marvelous book.

The first one is the key that I have already alluded to, but I want to develop it in more detail. The first key to understanding the Book of Revelation is for you to believe with all your heart that God wants you to understand it. I put this key first because you must approach the book with the right attitude if you hope to get anything out of it.

I can't emphasize too strongly the importance of this psychological breakthrough that must take place. You *must* believe that God wants you to understand. You've got to stop writing the book off as an intellectual exercise for theologians or as a fantasy for fanatics. No, it is for the average Christian. Better yet, it is for all Christians. That means it is for you, if you're a child of God. And it's for you to understand.

A Revelation of Jesus

Have you ever noticed that the Book of Revelation begins with a word of encouragement regarding the understanding of it? Consider Revelation 1:1: "The Revelation of Jesus Christ, which God gave Him to show to His bond servants, the things which must shortly take place; and He sent and communicated it by His angel to His bond-servant John." This is an encouraging verse. It affirms that God wants you to understand what is contained in the book.

Notice again the very first words: "The Revelation of Jesus Christ." The word, "revelation," is translated from the Greek word, "apocalypse," which means an unveiling. Isn't that interesting? The book begins by declaring that it is the unveiling or the uncovering or the revealing of Jesus Christ. It's no wonder that Satan doesn't want anybody reading it because the book focuses upon Jesus from the beginning to the end.

Let's go to Revelation 19, and I'll show you what I mean. In Revelation 19:10, which is one of my favorite verses in the book, we are told that "the testimony of Jesus is the spirit of prophecy." Prophecy focuses on Jesus. The Book of Revelation is prophetic literature. From start to finish it focuses upon Jesus Christ. It is the unveiling of Jesus. It shows His present glory and it discloses the greater glory that is yet to come. With a message like that, don't you think God wants you to understand what the book says?

God Desires to Communicate

Again, the first step is a psychological one. You must believe that God wants you to understand the book. Now, let me just reason with you here for a moment. Why would God write a book to you that He didn't want you to understand? Every book in the Bible is like a personal letter that God has written to you and me. He wants to communicate with us. He desires fellowship. He seeks communion. How do you have fellowship with somebody? The bottom line is that you've got to communicate with them.

God desires to talk with us. He wants us to communicate with Him through prayer and through the reading of His Word. God is not playing games with us. He didn't write the

Bible for doctoral students at seminaries. You don't have to
have degrees piled on top of degrees. In fact, you don't have
to have any degrees. The indispensable element is the indwelling power of God's Spirit.

The Necessity of the Holy Spirit

In this regard, the Book of Revelation is not a book for
unbelievers. Not at all. You know why? Because the Book of
Revelation is written in such a way that it cannot be understood unless the reader has the gift of the Holy Spirit. The
only way you'll understand the Book of Revelation is to lean
upon the illumination of the Holy Spirit. Let the Holy Spirit
be your teacher, and then you will understand it. Since only
Christians have the Holy Spirit, the unbeliever simply looks
at the Book of Revelation and considers it to be a bunch of
gobbledygook. It is beyond his grasp.

Unfortunately, this point applies to a lot of professing
Christians. I have in mind those who claim to be Christians
but who do not have the Holy Spirit living inside of them
because they've never really been born again. They're on a
church roll. They may have gone through some ordinance like
baptism. They may even teach in a seminary. But they never
have really been born again because they have no personal
relationship with Jesus Christ. Such persons cannot understand Revelation.

But I'm saying to you that every person on the face of
this earth who has truly been born again and thus has the
indwelling power of the Holy Spirit can understand the book.

Relying on the Holy Spirit

Relying on the Spirit for understanding God's Word is a
fundamental truth of the Bible. You must rely upon the Holy
Spirit and not your own intellectual powers.

Let me give you an example of what I'm talking about.
In 1 Corinthians 2 Paul makes this point over and over. He
says that Christians do not speak the wisdom of the world;
rather, we speak God's wisdom. He then hastens to point out

that God's wisdom is a mystery. It's a "hidden wisdom," which God predestined before the beginning of the world, and Paul says it is a wisdom that comes only to those who have the Spirit of God. In verse 10 of chapter 2 he says, "For to us God revealed [His secrets] through the Spirit; for the Spirit searches all things, even the depths of God." In verse 11 he adds, "The thoughts of God no one knows except the Spirit of God."

Paul then makes the point I am driving at. It is found in 1 Corinthians 2:12 — "Now we have received, not the spirit of the world, but the Spirit who is from God, that we may know the things freely given to us by God." He sums up the point in verse 16 where he says that because we have the Spirit, "we have the mind of Christ." What is Paul saying? He is teaching us that only through the Spirit of God can we understand the mysteries of God.

God's Greatest Teacher

The apostle John makes the same point in chapter 2 of his first epistle. In verse 20 he says that we have "an anointing from the Holy One." In verse 27 he observes that this anointing is the key to our understanding of Scripture because the Holy Spirit is our teacher. Here's how he puts it: "As for you, the anointing which you received from Him abides in you, and you have no need for anyone to teach you; but as His anointing teaches you about all things, and is true and not a lie, and just as it has taught you, you abide in Him" (1 John 2:27).

What John is saying here is that the Holy Spirit is our ultimate teacher of Scripture. The Holy Spirit can work in many different ways. He can work directly upon the believer, witnessing to his spirit (Rom. 8:16). He can work through the Word of God. He can work through a gospel singer or through a minister preaching a sermon or through a teaching lesson on a cassette tape. The Holy Spirit is the teacher of God. Accordingly, if you learn anything from this book, it's only because I've put myself aside and allowed the Spirit to fill me to the point that God can speak through me to you and to your spirit, enabling you to open your eyes to some of the mysteries of God.

Think of it this way. The Holy Spirit is the one who wrote the Bible. Every book of the Bible from Genesis to Revelation was written by the same person — by the Holy Spirit of God. Who better can teach you than the Spirit who wrote the book? So lean on the Holy Spirit within you and rely upon the Spirit to teach you what God's Word means.

Deciphering Symbols

Please don't be deceived by those people who come along and say, "But the Book of Revelation is apocalyptic; therefore, you can't understand it." That's a bunch of nonsense — just nonsense. I heard that for years. "It's apocalyptic! It's apocalyptic!" The word scared me to death. It sounded like a disease.

All the term means is that the Book of Revelation is a type of prophetic literature that uses a lot of symbols. Because it contains so many symbols, some people teach the book as if it were a sort of Alice-in-Wonderland story for adults. Part of that approach is to explain away the vivid picture images by spiritualizing them to mean anything the teacher desires. The only limit is the imagination. This is an unsound approach.

Keep in mind that symbols are used for a specific purpose. They stand for something. They have a literal meaning behind them. They were not selected pell-mell by the Holy Spirit when He inspired the book, and they do not stand for just anything we may desire.

Take Jesus, for example. In the Bible He is referred to as the "Rose of Sharon" (Song of Sol. 2:1). Now Jesus is not a rose, but the statement that He's the "Rose of Sharon" communicates something real about Him. It tells us that He's beautiful, that He's glorious, that He's wonderful, that He's the spiritual aroma of God. He's also called the "Bread of Life" and the "Fountain of Life." Each of these symbols is used to emphasize a different facet of His character. Think how improper it would be to refer to Him as "the Tumbleweed of Texas"! That symbol conjures up the image of something that is ugly and rootless, subject to every whim of the wind.

The same is true of symbols all through the Bible. When a symbol is used, always look for the literal meaning behind it. God does not use symbols randomly, just pulling them out of the sky as if they have no meaning whatsoever.

Using First Coming Prophecies as a Guide

If you will look at apocalyptic books in the Old Testament, like the Book of Zechariah, you will see that the First Coming prophecies contained in this literature meant exactly what they said. This is an extremely important point because the way in which First Coming prophecies were fulfilled is the best clue to how Second Coming prophecies will be fulfilled.

Let's consider some examples from the Book of Zechariah. The prophet said that the Messiah would come on a donkey and that He would ride into Jerusalem on that donkey (Zech. 9:9). Now, I'm sure that some of our liberal theologians today, if they had lived back before the coming of Christ, would have taken that verse and said, "Well, of course, this verse doesn't mean what it says. This is apocalyptic literature. All apocalyptic literature must be spiritualized. The Messiah certainly isn't coming on a donkey. That's silly. All the verse means is that He's going to be a humble person." Wrong. The verse meant what it said. Jesus came on a donkey, exactly as prophesied in apocalyptic literature (Matt. 21:1–9).

Zechariah also prophesied that the Messiah would be betrayed by a friend (Zech. 13:6) for 30 pieces of silver (Zech. 11:12). He said the Messiah would be pierced (Zech. 12:10) and that He would have wounds in His hands (Zech. 13:6). All these prophecies proved to be literal rather than symbolic.

Concerning the Messiah's second coming, Zechariah said He will come back to the Mount of Olives and the mountain will split in half when His foot touches the ground (Zech. 14:4). The Messiah will speak a supernatural word, destroying the Antichrist and his forces with a plague (Zech. 4:12). And in Zechariah 14:9 it says, "On that day the Lord will become king over all the earth." I believe those words mean exactly what they say. It is wrong to spiritualize them by arguing that they have a symbolic meaning, rather than a literal one.

Accepting the Plain Sense

Another key to understanding the Book of Revelation, a very important key, is to accept the plain sense meaning of each passage. Even if you don't understand it, the best rule of thumb is to just accept the plain sense meaning. My "Golden Rule of Interpretation" that I use throughout the Bible from beginning to end, whether it's prophecy or not, is this: "If the plain sense makes sense, don't look for any other sense, or you will end up with nonsense."

Because I realize that prophetic literature contains symbols, I don't like to use the term, "literal interpretation." I prefer the term, "plain sense interpretation." Yes, there are symbols, but symbols have meaning. And when symbols are used, I look for the meaning of them. Again, if the plain sense makes sense, don't look for any other sense, or you will end up with nonsense!

Remember, God doesn't write in riddles to purposefully confuse us. He knows how to communicate. Normally, He says what He means, and He means what He says. Try always to accept the plain sense meaning. If you don't understand it, don't worry about it. Put aside what is confusing and hang on to what you do understand. Don't give in to the temptation to spiritualize a passage to death or allegorize it. It is a serious thing to play loose with God's Word.

The spiritualization of Scripture is actually a blasphemous act. The reason is that when you start spiritualizing God's Word, you start playing god, for you can make the Scriptures mean whatever you want, rather than what God intended.

Believing When It's Difficult

The best commentary I have ever read on the Book of Revelation is one called *The Revelation Record* by Dr. Henry Morris.[2] Right at the very beginning he makes a statement that made me want to shout "Hallelujah!" He says, "The Book of Revelation is not hard to understand. It's just hard to believe. If you will believe it, you will understand it." What a profound insight! And it's so true. Don't forget it.

Accepting the plain sense meaning applies even when you don't understand the passage. Let me give you an example. In Revelation 9 it says that in the end times an army of 200 million is going to march out of the east toward Israel. At the time that was written there weren't even 200 million people in the world. Can you imagine the early readers of the book trying to figure out what that meant? Today, one nation, China, can send an army that large against Israel. You see what I mean by accepting what it says even if you don't understand it?

This is one of the reasons I have always held the writings of C. I. Scofield in high esteem. He is the man who in 1909 produced the very first study Bible — a Bible with explanatory notes.[3] He gave a literal interpretation to Ezekiel 38 and 39, concluding that these chapters prophesy that Russia, together with specified allies, will invade Israel in the end times. Commenting on this interpretation, he stated, "I don't understand it. I can't explain it. But that is what it says. Therefore, I believe it."

That statement required a lot of faith in the literal meaning of the Word of God. Think of it — in 1909 Russia was a Christian Orthodox nation and Israel did not exist, nor was there any prospect that Israel would ever exist!

The Impact of Technology

Modern technology has helped us to understand many prophecies that previously have been a mystery. For example, in Revelation 13 it says that when the Antichrist is revealed, he's going to be accompanied by a person known as the false prophet. This false prophet will make an image of the Antichrist, and that image will seem to come alive. People will worship the image. For thousands of years people have had to wonder what was meant by the reference to an image that appears to be alive. Scholars wrote many pages giving the passage all kinds of spiritualized explanations. Today, with the technology that we have, it is not at all difficult to make a robotic or digital image that appears to be alive.

Forty years ago I went into a theater at Disneyland. When the curtain opened, I saw a person who looked like Abe Lincoln sitting on the stage. He got up, walked over to the edge of the stage, grabbed his coat lapels, and proceeded to deliver the "Gettysburg Address." The person was so lifelike. I thought he was an actor. He wasn't. The person was a robot.

The Bible says the false prophet will make an image of the Antichrist that will appear to come alive. I think we should believe the Bible means what it says.

In the same chapter of Revelation, chapter 13, we are told that every person on earth during the Tribulation period will be required to have a mark of the beast (either his name or number) on their forehead or on their right hand in order to buy and sell. For centuries, this was a prophecy whose plain sense fulfillment was difficult to comprehend. But no longer. Today, with the kind of technology that we have with computers and lasers, such a mark is something that is readily possible. Nonetheless, until recently people just had to accept by faith that the passage meant what it said.

Another example is found in Revelation 11 where it says that during the Tribulation two great witnesses of God will testify for three and a half years. They will perform mighty miracles and then be killed by the Antichrist. Their bodies will lie in the streets of Jerusalem for three days, and it says all the people of the world will look upon them. Then, suddenly, they will be resurrected and taken up to heaven. Needless to say, before the Soviet Sputnik in 1957, that passage was difficult to explain. How could all the world look upon two dead bodies lying in the streets of Jerusalem? Today, there's nothing to it. All you do is take a TV camera, point it at them, and zap the transmission up to a satellite. Instantly, the whole world can look upon those bodies without any difficulty at all.

Summing It Up

People have spent centuries explaining away God's Word simply because they did not necessarily understand it. I'm saying take the plain sense approach. Assume that God wants to communicate, that God knows how to communicate, and that God says what He means and means what He says. Believe that symbols stand for something literal, and accept them for their plain sense meaning. You will start understanding the Book of Revelation.

Okay, we have covered four keys to understanding the prophecies of Revelation. First, believe God wants you to understand. Second, rely on the Holy Spirit to be your teacher. Third, remember that symbols stand for something literal. Fourth, accept the plain sense meaning, even if it is not fully understandable to you.

Following the Table of Contents

The fifth key to understanding relates to the book's table of contents. Yes, Revelation has a table of contents! This is a crucial point that many people have overlooked. Consulting the table of contents is essential to making sense out of the book.

Let's take a look at the table of contents. It's in Revelation 1:19. Jesus instructs John to do something: "Write therefore the things which you have seen, and the things which are, and the things which shall take place after these things."

Notice that Jesus told John to write down three things: first, the things which he had seen; second, the things which existed at that time; and third, the things which would take place in the future. That is the table of contents of the Book of Revelation.

Now, let's relate these three sections to the book itself. The things which John had seen are recorded in chapter 1. He saw the astonishing appearance of the risen Lord on the Island of Patmos. John saw Jesus in all of His resurrection glory. Chapter 1 is the first section of the book referred to in Revelation 1:19. It is "the things which you have seen."

The second section of the table of contents is "the things which are" — that is, the things that existed in that day and time. That corresponds to chapters 2 and 3, the letters to the seven churches of Asia. Those seven letters represent the Church as it existed at the end of the first century.

From chapter 4 through the end of the book you have the future, "the things which shall take place after these things." You say, "Well, how do you know this section begins with chapter 4?" Consider chapter 4, verse 1: "After these things I looked, and behold, a door standing open in heaven, and the first voice which I heard, like the sound of a trumpet speaking with me, said, 'Come up here, and I will show you what *must take place after these things.'* " Notice that this verse ends with the exact wording contained in Revelation 1:19 regarding "the things that must take place after these things." And so, from chapter 4 through the end of the book you have the future, the end-time events.

Mark the table of contents in your Bible. Write the following summary at the beginning of the book so that you will have it for easy reference:

1) "the things which you have seen" — the glorified Jesus — chapter 1.

2) "the things which are" — the seven churches — chapters 2 and 3.

3) "the things which shall take place after these things" — the Tribulation, the Millennium, and the eternal state — chapter 4 through the end of the book.

Watching the Time Frame

The sixth key is to watch the time frame of what you are reading. This is probably the most ignored key to understanding the book. Yet, it is vitally important.

Watching the time frame is important when reading any type of literature. The Book of Revelation in this regard is no different from a novel. When you are reading a novel, you always have to be aware of the time frame of the passage that you are reading. Is it in the past, the present, or the future?

For example, you might come across a flashback as you are reading a novel. Suddenly, you are transported back in time to something that happened years ago. Then, you might be propelled right back to the present and read some events that are just occurring in the story line of the book. The book might even contain a flash-forward.

Flash-forwards are not as common in regular secular literature as they are in spiritual literature. The Bible is full of flash-forwards because God knows what's going to happen in the future and, through the revelation of His Holy Spirit, He gives supernatural knowledge to His prophets concerning future events.

The flash-forward is a very common literary device in the Book of Revelation. Although the Book of Revelation is set up in chronological order in the sense that the major events it portrays occur one after the other, nevertheless, there are many places in its story line where it flashes forward to events that are going to occur in the future. You must be very sensitive to this if you are to understand what is going on in the book.

Time Frame Changes

Let me give you some examples of passages in Revelation that contain flashbacks or flash-forwards. When you reach the end of Revelation 11 you are in the middle of the Tribulation. The Antichrist has just been revealed, and he has murdered the two great prophets of God who have been preaching repentance for three and a half years. As Revelation 12 begins, the action of the story line halts with a flashback that is designed to tell the reader why the Antichrist is raging against God and His saints.

The first five verses of Revelation 12 tell the story in symbolic language of how Israel gave birth to the Messiah and how Satan tried to kill Him at birth. The point of this flashback is that Satan hates Israel with a special passion because the Jewish people were the ones through whom God provided the Messiah.

Verse six ends the flashback by resuming the story line. It tells us that a remnant of the Jewish people will flee into the wilderness in the middle of the Tribulation to escape the wrath of the Antichrist. The rest of chapter 12 is in the present tense time frame, describing events that occur at the middle of the Tribulation, such as Satan's attempt to take the throne of God one last time, resulting in a war in heaven.

Chapter 13 continues the present tense time frame. It describes in detail some of the initial activities of the Antichrist and his false prophet after they come to power. While the Antichrist makes war on the saints and exerts his authority over all the world, his false prophet sets up a blasphemous religious system and a totalitarian society.

The present tense action comes to a halt once again with the beginning of chapter 14. This time the action is interrupted by a flash-forward that is designed to comfort the reader by assuring him that despite all the terrible actions of the Antichrist and his false prophet, Jesus Christ will triumph. Verse 1 reads, "And I looked, and behold, the Lamb was standing on Mount Zion, and with Him one hundred and forty-four thousand, having His name and the name of His Father written on their foreheads." This is a flash-forward to the end of the Tribulation. The Lamb, Jesus Christ, has come. He is standing on Mount Zion in Jerusalem. He is accompanied by a host of Jewish evangelists who were sealed by God at the beginning of the Tribulation.

All the rest of chapter 14 is a flash-forward. It takes the form of a preview at the movies, telling us in abbreviated form what lies ahead. Verses 6 through 20 give us a panoramic over-view of the rest of the events that are yet to take place in the final days of the Tribulation. For example, verse 8 tells us about the fall of "Babylon the great." That fall does not take place in the present tense time frame until chapter 18.

Tricky Flash-Forwards

Flash-forwards like the ones in Revelation 14 are the most difficult of the time frames to catch. We are not accus-tomed to these in secular literature, and we tend to overlook them when reading the Bible. As you become familiar with prophetic literature, you will be able to spot these flash-for-ward passages more easily. This is particularly true of the Book of Revelation because the book has a certain rhythm to it. Part of that rhythm is periodic pauses designed to en-courage the reader. These pauses almost always consist of flash-forwards.

Flash-forwards are given in the Book of Revelation pri-marily for one reason: to give comfort to the reader. There are so many horrible events revealed in the book regarding the pouring out of the wrath of man, the wrath of Satan, and the wrath of God that every once in a while the writer seems com-pelled to stop and give a flash-forward to the end of the Tribu-lation to assure the reader that Jesus Christ is going to be com-pletely victorious.

For example, chapters 8 and 9 describe in vivid, horrify-ing detail how one-third of humanity is going to die in the second set of judgments (the trumpet judgments) that will be poured out during the first half of the Tribulation. By the time the reader gets to the end of chapter 9, the scene on earth is so terrible that some encouragement is needed. That en-couragement is supplied by chapter 10 which is a flash-for-ward to the second coming of Jesus who is portrayed as a "strong angel." Through the testimony of chapter 10 the reader is assured that everything is going to turn out all right when Jesus returns.

A Pause to Review

Let's review our keys to understanding the Book of Revelation once again. First, believe God wants you to understand. Second, rely on the Holy Spirit. Third, look for the literal meaning of symbols. Fourth, accept the plain sense meaning of what you are reading. Fifth, follow the table of contents outlined in Revelation 1:19. Sixth, watch the time frame of what you are reading — is it past, present, or future?

Studying the Old Testament

The seventh key is the study of the Old Testament. I grew up in a church which, like most Protestant churches, just studied the New Testament. We rarely ever even read the Old Testament, much less studied it.

After 30 years of faithful church attendance, I was biblically ignorant concerning the Old Testament. I couldn't have found the Book of Zephaniah without an index if my life had depended on it. I would have been embarrassed to discover that there was no book of Hezekiah. I had been told over and over again that "the Old Testament was nailed to the Cross." Accordingly, I considered the Old Testament to be irrelevant.

In view of such ignorance of the Old Testament — a condition that is common throughout Christendom — it is no wonder that the average Christian has so much difficulty understanding New Testament prophecy like the Book of Revelation. We don't know Old Testament prophecy, yet it is the key to understanding the prophecies in the New Testament. Old Testament prophecy fits together with New Testament prophecy like a hand in a glove. There is no way, for example, that you will ever understand Revelation if you are not thoroughly familiar with Daniel.

I finally got to a point in my study of the Book of Revelation where I just could not advance in my understanding until I went back to the Old Testament and began to study the major and minor prophets. As I began to absorb the writings of these prophets, I began to understand the Book of Revelation like I had never understood it before.

Old Testament Testimony

Let me give you an example of what I'm talking about. There's a statement I must have heard dozens of times from the pulpit when I was growing up: "There's only one chapter in the Bible that speaks of a future reign of Jesus Christ, and that's Revelation chapter 20." Many preachers would go on to draw the incredible conclusion that since only one chapter mentions a future reign of the Lord on the earth, it must mean something else! They would then proceed to spiritualize away the plain sense meaning of Revelation 20, denying that the Lord will ever return to the earth to reign.

You can imagine how shocked I was to discover later on that the Old Testament contains over five hundred prophecies about the second coming of Jesus, many of which relate specifically to His reign on earth. There are three hundred prophecies about His first coming, but over five hundred about His second coming. There is prophecy after prophecy about the return of Jesus to this earth to reign in glory and majesty from Jerusalem. Revelation 20 is *not* the only place in the Bible that speaks of a future reign of Jesus Christ. It is one chapter out of many that focus on the future reign of the Lord.

The Affirmation of Isaiah

An example of Old Testament prophecy pointing to the reign of Jesus is found in Isaiah 24, beginning with verse 21. Speaking of the end times, Isaiah says, "So it will happen in that day, that the Lord will punish the host of heaven on high, and the kings of the earth, on the earth." Who is "the host of heaven on high"? That's Satan and his demonic hordes who, we are told in Ephesians 6, infest the atmosphere of this planet. The Lord is going to punish them in the heavens.

Now notice where He is going to punish the kings of this world — "on the earth." Verse 22 says, "They will be gathered together like prisoners in a dungeon, and will be confined in prison." That's speaking of *sheol* or hades, the holding place for the spirits of the unrighteous dead.

What this passage is saying is that when the Lord comes

back, He's going to pour out His wrath. He's going to consign to death all those who have rejected him as Lord and Savior. Their spirits will be confined in prison. They will be put in hades. Then, "after many days" (the thousand year reign of Jesus), they will be punished, because at the end of the Millennium, they will be resurrected, judged, and cast into hell.

Continuing with verse 23, Isaiah writes, "Then the moon will be abashed and the sun ashamed, for the Lord will reign." Where? In heaven? No. He will reign "on Mount Zion and in Jerusalem." That's a geographical location on planet Earth.

I don't know what God would have to do to convince us that Jesus is going to reign in Jerusalem. He says so very plainly right here in this passage from Isaiah. He even tells us one of the purposes of the Lord's reign. Consider again verse 23. Isaiah says the Lord will "manifest His glory before His elders." Jesus was humiliated in history the first time He came. When He returns, He will receive honor and glory.

Other Old Testament Examples

Another example of Second Coming prophecy in the Old Testament can be found in the third chapter of the Book of Joel, one of those so-called minor prophets (minor in length, not in content!). Joel speaks in verse 14 of the Battle of Armageddon: "Multitudes, multitudes in the valley of decision! For the day of the Lord is near in the valley of decision. The sun and moon grow dark and the stars lose their brightness." And what happens? "The Lord roars from Zion and utters His voice from Jerusalem, and the heavens and the earth tremble. But the Lord is a refuge for His people and a stronghold to the sons of Israel." He adds, "Then you will know that I am the Lord your God." When? When He is "dwelling in Zion, My holy mountain." The Book of Joel ends with the Lord returning like a lion to pour out His wrath on the enemies of God and to dwell in Zion — in Jerusalem. What could be clearer?

One of the most powerful and inspirational passages in the Old Testament concerning the coming reign of Jesus is to be found in the fourth chapter of Micah. It begins in verse 1 with these words: "It will come about in the last days that the mountain of the house of the Lord, will be established as the chief of the mountains." In Bible prophecy the word "mountain" is a symbol for a kingdom, unless the mountain is specifically named. Thus, the first words of this prophecy point to a kingdom of the Lord that will be established in the last days, a kingdom that will be the chief of all kingdoms on this earth. "It will be raised up above the hills" — the nations — "and the peoples will stream to it."

As Micah's prophecy continues, he identifies the geographical location of the Lord's kingdom: "Many nations will come and say, 'Come and let us go up to the mountain of the Lord and to the house of the God of Jacob, that He may teach us about His ways and that we may walk in His paths.' For from Zion will go forth the law, even the word of the Lord from Jerusalem." Again, the geographical location of the kingdom is made crystal clear, and it is here on this earth.

The prophecy continues with inspiring images of the peace and prosperity that will flood the earth during the Lord's reign. It concludes in verse 7 with these words: "The Lord will reign over them in Mount Zion, from now on and forever." Where will the Lord reign? In heaven? No. On Mount Zion. That's Jerusalem.

These examples from Old Testament prophecy make it abundantly clear how foolish it is to say that Revelation 20 is the only chapter in the Bible that mentions an earthly reign of the Lord. The lesson is apparent. Old Testament prophecy is indispensable to an understanding of New Testament prophecy.

Paying a Price

That means you are going to have to pay a price to understand Bible prophecy. The price is study. But this is no different from any other area of spiritual growth. God never zaps anybody with spiritual maturity. You always have to pay a price. The price is worn-out Bibles and calluses on the knees.

You've got to get into God's Word — *all of it.* You've also got to spend a lot of time in prayer.

Getting into the Old Testament is particularly important when it comes to understanding the Book of Revelation. The reason is that Revelation has over three hundred quotations in it from the Old Testament, more than any other book in the New Testament. Revelation is saturated with Old Testament thought and quotes. But the amazing thing is that not one of those quotations is specifically mentioned!

Do you understand what I mean? Take the Book of Matthew, for example. Matthew is the gospel to the Jews, and as such, it has a lot of quotations from Old Testament prophecy. But every time Matthew quotes the Old Testament, he specifically identifies the quote and the source. Thus, when Jesus left Nazareth and moved to Capernaum, Matthew wrote, "This was to fulfill what was spoken through Isaiah the prophet, saying," — and he then proceeds to quote Isaiah 9:1. (See Matt. 4:14–16.)

The Old Testament in Revelation

Like Matthew, the Book of Revelation contains quote after quote from the Old Testament. But unlike Matthew, Revelation never once identifies any quote as a quotation, nor does it identify the source. If you did not know Old Testament prophecy, you could read the whole Book of Revelation and never be aware that it had ever once quoted the Old Testament. But it quotes it or alludes to it over three hundred times.

Let me give you an example. Go back to the theme that we looked at earlier, Revelation 1:7 — "Behold, He is coming with the clouds, and every eye will see Him, even those who pierced Him; and all the tribes of the earth will mourn over Him. So it is to be, Amen." As I pointed out before, this is a very important verse because it expresses the theme of the whole book.

What most people do not realize, because there is no clue in the text, is that this verse is a fusion of two quotes from the

Old Testament. One of the verses is from Daniel 7:13: "Behold, with the clouds of heaven One like a Son of Man was coming. . . ." The other verse is from Zechariah 12:10: "They will look on Me whom they have pierced; and they will mourn for Him, as one mourns for an only son." The writer just puts those two together and quotes them as if he's not even quoting, as if he's making up the words as he goes along. But anyone familiar with Old Testament prophecy will immediately recognize the sources of this verse.

How do you understand the Book of Revelation? First, believe God wants you to understand it. Second, rely on the Holy Spirit to teach you. Third, look for the literal meaning of symbols. Fourth, accept the plain sense meaning. Fifth, follow the table of contents, Revelation 1:19. Sixth, watch the time frame of what you're reading. Seventh, study the Old Testament, especially the prophetic literature.

Focusing on Jesus

The eighth key is to keep your eyes on Jesus. This is a point that I simply can't emphasize enough. Look again at the very first verse of Revelation: "This is the Revelation of Jesus Christ." From beginning to end, it is the revelation of Jesus.

There are so many prophecy teachers who ignore this truth. You've seen their ads in the newspaper. The ads are usually decorated with weird pictures of beasts with seven heads. And the ads are full of tantalizing questions. "Does Bill Clinton's name add up to 666? Is Henry Kissinger the false prophet? Is there a computer beast in Belgium? Are the vultures gathering in Jerusalem?" Such teachers specialize in the sensational. They focus on anything but Jesus Christ.

It's no wonder so many people have washed their hands of Bible prophecy, having decided it's a playground for fanatics. Unfortunately, it is a playground for a lot of fanatics, but it doesn't have to be that. It can be green pastures for disciples, if you keep your eyes on Jesus.

When you read the Book of Revelation, look for Jesus.

Remember that — *look for Jesus!* The more you look for Him, the more you're going to see Him. And if you will keep your eyes focused on Jesus, you will understand the Book of Revelation. Again, Revelation 19:10 says point blank, "the testimony of Jesus is the spirit of prophecy."

Jesus himself emphasized this point to His disciples. During the 40 days between His resurrection and His ascension, He went through the Hebrew Scriptures with His disciples to show them "that all things which are written about Me in the law of Moses and the Prophets and the Psalms must be fulfilled" (Luke 24:44).

Interpretive Approaches

We have surveyed eight major keys to understanding Revelation. There is one more piece of unfinished business yet to cover before we launch into an overview of the book, chapter by chapter. We must look at the most important systems of interpretation that have developed historically to explain the meaning of the book.

Following the eight keys I have outlined above will produce what is called a futurist interpretation of the book. The futurist approach is one of four systems of interpretation that have developed in response to the book. Let's take a brief look at all four.[4]

The Futurist

The first interpretive approach to develop was the futurist. This is the school of thought that views all of Revelation following chapter 4 to be prophecy that will be fulfilled in the future. In other words, the vast majority of the book is considered to be prophecy that will not be fulfilled until the end times when the Lord returns.

This futurist view is the one that was held by the Early Church fathers. We know this for certain because it is the only view that is expressed in their writings in the first two centuries after Christ.[5] Papias (c. 130), who served as the bishop of Phrygian Hieropolis, argued that the Millennium would be a future golden age on earth.[6] Other Early Church fathers, like Irenaeus (c. 130–202), Tertullian (c. 160–240), and Lactantius (c. 250–330), also endorsed the futurist interpretation.[7] Justin Martyr (c. 100–165), the foremost defender of the faith in the second century, indicated there were other viewpoints, but he stated forthrightly that the futurist view was the predominant and orthodox one: "I and others, who are right-minded Christians on all points, are assured that there will be a resurrection of the dead, and a thousand years in Jerusalem, which will then be built, adorned and enlarged, as the prophets Ezekiel and Isaiah and others declare."[8]

The futurist view was set aside by the Roman Catholic Church in A.D. 431 at the Council of Ephesus when it endorsed a new interpretive approach which was systematized and popularized by St. Augustine in his book *The City of God.*

The Historicist View

Augustine (354–430) refined what came to be known as the historicist approach. Based upon a spiritualization of Scripture, this viewpoint argued that the prophecies of Revelation applied to contemporary historical developments and not to some distant future period called "the end times."[9]

Augustine saw the prophecies being fulfilled in the Church in the current church age. Thus, to him the Tribulation represented the struggle of the Church against the Roman Empire. The seven-year length of the Tribulation was not interpreted as meaning a literal seven-year period. Rather, the number was taken to symbolize a complete period of time known only to God but subsequently revealed in history as the time from the establishment of the Church to the conversion of Constantine in A.D. 312.

The beast or Antichrist was the Roman Empire. The false prophet was the council of the Empire entrusted with the enforcement of emperor worship. The conversion of the emperor to Christianity was viewed as the Lord's triumph over the Antichrist. With that triumph, the Millennium had begun, with Jesus reigning over the world through the Church. The

New Jerusalem was interpreted to be a symbol of the Church's governing glory. These highly spiritualized interpretations make it easy to understand why the view gained such quick popularity among Church leaders.

But this interpretive approach was to backfire on the Catholic Church when it was adopted and rewritten 1,200 years later by the leaders of the Reformation.[10] The Reformers took the position that the prophecies of Revelation applied to the Roman Catholic Church in a different way — not to its triumph over the Roman Empire, but to its apostasy. They argued that the Book of Revelation is a prophecy about the Church's growing apostasy, its struggle against true believers, and its ultimate discipline by the wrath of God. The Antichrist was, of course, the papacy, and the false prophet represented the Church's instruments of enforcement, like the Inquisition. This is the viewpoint I grew up with. Our preachers used Revelation primarily to bash the Catholic Church.

The historicist view has many variations, but the one thing that characterizes all the variations is a belief that most of the Book of Revelation has been fulfilled in history. It was fulfilled either in the conflict between the Church and the Roman Empire, between the reformers and the Catholic Church, or it is being fulfilled now in the conflict between the Church and the world.[11]

During the 20th century the historicist view died out, being replaced primarily by a resurgence of the futurist approach. Eugene Boring, in his commentary on Revelation, summarizes this phenomenon as follows: "Although widely held by Protestant interpreters after the Reformation and into the twentieth century, no critical New Testament scholar today advocates this view."[12] The only well-known prophecy teacher who utilizes this viewpoint today is Irvin Baxter Jr.[13]

The Preterist View

The third system of interpretation was developed in response to the historicist view of the reformers. It is called the preterist viewpoint.[14] That's a rather strange name. It comes from a Latin word meaning past tense. The word is appropriate because this view holds that either all or most of the Book of Revelation was fulfilled in the first century!

The view was developed in the 17th century by a Jesuit priest named Luis de Alcazar (1554–1613).[15] His purpose was to defend the Catholic Church against the attacks of the reformers. He denied the reformers' charge that the Book of Revelation was a prophecy about the apostasy of the Roman Church. Instead, he argued that the book was a prophecy about the Church's struggles during its early years. Chapters 4 through 11 were interpreted as depicting the Church's fight against Judaism, culminating in the fall of Jerusalem in A.D. 70. Chapters 12 through 19 were viewed as the Church's struggle against paganism, ending with the fall of Rome in 476. Chapters 20 through 22 were interpreted to be a symbolic description of the glories of papal Rome. Using this clever approach, Alcazar was able to limit the range of Revelation's prophecies to the first 500 years of the Christian Era.

Alcazar was a mild preterist. A more radical form of preterism gained popularity in the latter part of the 20th century and is today the most widely held version of this interpretive approach.[16] It sees nearly all the prophecies of Revelation as fulfilled in the A.D. 70 destruction of Jerusalem, except for the resurrection of believers and the second coming of Jesus. It assigns the Tribulation to the fall of Israel, the great apostasy to the first century Church, and the last days to the period between Jesus' ascension and the destruction of Jerusalem. The beast is viewed as a symbol of Nero in particular and the Roman Empire in general. The false prophet is equated with the leadership of apostate Israel. Needless to say, many of the spokesmen for this viewpoint are anti-Semitic.

There is a more extreme form of preterism whose advocates consider themselves to be "consistent preterists."[17] They take the position that all so-called "end-time prophecy" was fulfilled in the destruction of Jerusalem in A.D. 70 — including the Second Coming and the resurrection of believers! They do not look forward to any future resurrection or any end of history. They believe we are currently living in the eternal state.

The Idealist View

The fourth system of interpretation is called the idealist view. It is the viewpoint of most theological liberals. The father of this approach is considered to be William Milligan who developed the viewpoint in a book that he wrote in 1889.[18]

This view advocates that the Book of Revelation is a type of adult "Alice-in-Wonderland" story containing vivid word pictures that do not have any particular or specific meaning. They spiritualize the book to death. Their conclusion is that the Book of Revelation is simply a fairy tale in which God uses vivid images to teach one fundamental lesson: good will triumph over evil. "According to this view, the great themes of the triumph of good over evil, of Christ over Satan, of the vindication of the martyrs and the sovereignty of God are played out throughout Revelation without necessary reference to single historical events."[19]

There are a few Idealists who attempt to relate their interpretation to history in general. They fall into the idealist school rather than the historicist because they avoid linking the prophecies of Revelation to specific historical events. A classic example is William Hendriksen's 1939 book *More Than Conquerors*. He relates Revelation to the history of the entire Church Age but, as he puts it, "The symbols refer not to specific events, particular happenings, or details of history, but to principles — of human conduct and of divine moral government — that are operating throughout the history of the world, especially throughout the new dispensation."[20]

An Eclectic Approach

My own viewpoint is eclectic in nature because it consists of a combination of all the views outlined above. I can agree with the preterists when they insist that the Book of

Revelation contained a message of encouragement to first century Christians, assuring them that the Church would ultimately triumph over the Roman Empire. I can also relate to the Reformation historicists when they argue that the prophecies of Revelation relate to the corruption of the Roman Church and its persecution of true believers.

In other words, I believe the Book of Revelation has always had a continuing relevance as a source of encouragement to suffering Christians throughout the history of the Church. It has always served as a reminder that the Church will ultimately triumph over all its oppressors.

That's why I can even agree with the liberal, idealist viewpoint when it argues that the ultimate message of the book is that good will triumph over evil. How can anyone argue with that conclusion when the book clearly teaches that Satan will be crushed and Jesus will emerge totally triumphant?

But I also believe in the futurist view that most of the Book of Revelation is yet to be fulfilled and is to be fulfilled in its plain sense meaning. In other words, I believe there's going to be a real Antichrist and not just a symbolic Antichrist. Yes, there have been symbolic antichrists in the past, but there is going to be a fulfillment in a literal Antichrist in the future. I also believe the Tribulation, Millennium, and eternal state are all yet future.

Relating the Views to Each Other

As I look at these four systems of interpretation and consider their relationship to each other, I am reminded of how an overhead projector works. You can put a transparency on the projector that shows the land of Israel in the time of Joshua. Then you can lay on top of that transparency another one that shows the boundaries of the land at the time of Jesus. Another overlay could show the land's boundaries during the time of the Crusaders. A final overlay could outline the boundaries as they exist today. Each transparency contains an element of truth about the land. The light shines through all the transparencies to give you the full picture, showing you how the boundaries have changed over the years.

I think that's the way these schools of interpretation relate to each other. Each one of the four contains an element of truth. The problem comes when you accept only one and reject all the others. We must never forget that the Book of Revelation contained a very relevant message to first century Christians. It assured them of their ultimate victory over the Roman Empire. We must also remember that the book has been given relevant application to the struggles of the Church throughout history.

Looking to the Future

But we must also keep in mind that the futurist view is correct when it says that the ultimate fulfillment of the book's prophecies is yet future.

There really is going to be a seven-year period of Tribulation. A Jewish temple is going to be rebuilt in Jerusalem. A real person empowered by Satan will march into that temple, blaspheme God, and declare himself to be a god. This Antichrist will become the scourge of the earth. He will attempt to exterminate the Jewish people. Just as he appears to be on the verge of victory in accomplishing this satanic goal, the Lord Jesus will break from the heavens with all His holy ones, returning to the Mount of Olives in Jerusalem from which He ascended into heaven. The Lord will crush the Antichrist and inaugurate the greatest kingdom the world has ever known. The earth will be flooded with peace, righteousness, and justice — as the waters cover the sea.

An Outline

And now, before we begin our pilgrimage through the Book of Revelation, I want to present you with an outline and a challenge. Let's consider the outline first.

The Book of Revelation may be outlined in many different ways. Every outline I've ever seen has given me some insight into the book. I want to give you a very simple outline.

By focusing on Jesus, we can divide the book into four major parts. In chapters 1 through 3 you have Jesus in the Church Age. The focus is upon the Church and Jesus among His churches, encouraging them to be faithful to Him. Chapters 4 through 18 focus upon Jesus in the Tribulation, pouring out the wrath of God on those who have rejected God's love and grace. Chapters 19 through 20 present Jesus in His kingdom. He returns to earth in chapter 19 and establishes His kingdom. Chapter 20 presents His thousand-year reign. Finally, chapters 21 and 22 present us with Jesus in eternity. They give us a glimpse of the eternal state when we will live in glorified bodies on a new earth in the presence of God the Father, God the Son, and God the Holy Spirit.

To summarize:

Chapters 1–3:   Jesus in His church
Chapters 4–18:   Jesus in the Tribulation
Chapters 19–20:   Jesus in His kingdom
Chapters 21–22:   Jesus in eternity

A Challenge

I want to challenge you to do something before you read the rest of this book. My challenge is for you to stop at this point and read the Book of Revelation. Get a good modern translation like the New King James or the New American Standard or the New International and read the Book of Revelation all the way through at one sitting without any interruptions. You might even try reading it aloud to someone in your family or to a friend.

Don't try to figure out every fine point of it. Don't worry about the parts you don't understand. Don't even read it for understanding. Just read it for the purpose of allowing the Spirit of God to speak through it to your spirit. Read it for a spiritual blessing. Remember to pray at the beginning that God will give you the spiritual blessing of understanding. Claim Revelation 1:3 in prayer.

People spend a lot of time reading books *about* the Book

of Revelation and very little time reading the Revelation it-self. Read the Revelation. Read it from chapter 1 through chapter 22 in one sitting. Pray first and then just sit back and let the Holy Spirit bless your socks off, because He'll do it through this mighty and glorious book.

I look forward to walking with you through the Book of Revelation in the next chapter. I look forward to sharing thoughts with you about this marvelous book. I pray that God will use me as an instrument through whom the Holy Spirit can give you insights that will literally draw you into a closer relationship with Jesus.

If you are a believer, I pray our pilgrimage will motivate you to holiness in preparation for the Lord's soon return. I pray too that it will create within you an evangelistic fervor to share the truth of Jesus with other people.

If you are an unbeliever, I pray that this study will bring you to repentance in Jesus so that you might be delivered from the wrath of God to the glory of Jesus.

Chapter 2

Interpreting Revelation

W hat is the identity of the two witnesses of God who will be killed by the Antichrist? What will be the nationality of the Antichrist? Will the capital city of the Antichrist's kingdom be Rome or Babylon? What is the meaning of the mysterious number, 666?

When studying the Book of Revelation, most people seem to get bogged down in the details. Tragically, they often focus on the Antichrist rather than Jesus Christ. In the process they miss the big picture and the fundamental message.

The questions stated above are not unimportant — and many will be addressed in the next chapter of this book — but they pale in comparison to the overall message of Revelation.

So, let's go for the big picture, and let's seek the central biblical message. Let's engage in a sweeping overview of the book, chapter by chapter. As we begin, you should have the Book of Revelation handy for quick reference.

Chapter 1

The Writer

Now, who was this John? He does not clearly identify himself, but the testimony of all the Early Church fathers is that this was the apostle John.[1] All he says about himself is that he is a "brother and fellow partaker in the tribulation and kingdom and perseverance which are in Jesus" (Rev. 1:9).

I love the humility of that statement. If this man truly was the apostle John, as I believe he was, think of all the things he could have said about himself. He could have said, "This is John speaking to you; John the Apostle; John, the one who was a member of the Lord's inner circle; John, the one to whom the Lord gave the seat of honor at the Last Supper; John, the one to whom Jesus entrusted the care of His mother as He hung on the cross." John doesn't give us his credentials because he wants us to focus on the glorified Lord and not upon himself.

The Time

It is interesting that John was on the island of Patmos (Rev. 1:9). His imprisonment there is one of the clues to the dating of the book around A.D. 95 because that was when the Roman Empire turned against the Church. This happened because the Empire declared Caesar to be god, and every person in the Empire was required once a year to go before a Roman magistrate and declare, "Caesar is Lord!" No Christian could do that, and therefore Christians were considered enemies of the Empire. The result is that they became the target of terrible persecution.

With regard to timing, John tells us something very important in verse 10. He states that he was "in the Spirit on the Lord's day." Being "in the Spirit" can mean one of two things. It can refer to being under the control and guidance of the Spirit (Matt. 22:43), or it can refer to an experience of one's spirit that might even be apart from the body (2 Cor. 12:1–4). John refers three other times to being "in the Spirit" (Rev. 4:2, 17:3, and 21:10), all of which imply out-of-body experiences.

But the important thing is his reference to "the Lord's day." Commentators have often assumed that this is a reference to his experience occurring on Sunday. I personally do not believe this is what John was referring to. We know from the writings of the Church fathers that the term, "Lord's Day" did not become a synonym for Sunday until about 300 years later. When John mentions "the Lord's Day," I think he is referring to what the Hebrew prophets called "the Day of the Lord" (Joel 2:1), which was a term for the end times.

In Hebrew there is no adjective form of the word "Lord." Therefore, in Hebrew one must say, "the Day of the Lord." It is not possible to say "the Lord's Day." That is not true of the Greek language in which Revelation was written.

So, I believe John is telling us that "in the Spirit" he was catapulted forward to "the Day of the Lord" — to the end times — and given a preview of what will happen when the Church Age comes to a close.

The Need

John was about 95 years old when this book was written. He was the only apostle left alive, and he was a prisoner on the island of Patmos because of his testimony of Jesus Christ. What a powerful testimony he must have had for the Roman Empire to be so frightened of a 95-year-old man that they would put him in chains on a barren island!

The thing that you need to keep in mind is that by the time this book was written the persecution of Christians had become so terrible that it is evident from the Book of Revelation that many were wondering if the Church would really continue to exist. They were beginning to have second thoughts, wondering if Jesus really was who He said He was, wondering if Jesus really cared for them, wondering if He really meant it when He said, "Upon this rock I will build My church, and the gates of Hades will not overpower it" (Matt. 16:18).

The Church needed encouragement, and that's really one of the main purposes of the book. It is designed to give encouragement and comfort to those who are suffering terribly. For that reason, the Book of Revelation has always been a book that has given tremendous comfort to anyone going through persecution or suffering, whether it be individual, family, or national in nature.

The Appearance

The book begins, therefore, with a tremendous vision of Jesus Christ, the glorified One. He is victorious over death, and the heavenly glory which He surrendered when He came to earth (Phil. 2:5–8) has been restored. John sees Jesus resurrected and glorified. Keep in mind that this is 65 years after the death, burial, and resurrection of the Lord. Jesus has returned to give the Church a second touch, a touch of encouragement. He has returned to say, "Yes, I care. I love you. I know what's going on. I'm walking among you."

In verses 12 through 17 John describes Jesus in His glorified form. He sees Jesus dressed as a priest because that's what Jesus is now. He is our high priest before the throne of God, our mediator before God (Heb. 8:1–2). John sees Jesus with white hair, which indicates His purity and wisdom. His eyes, feet, and voice are all presented as symbols of judgment because all judgment has been given to Him by the Father (John 5:22). He has stars in His right hand which are "the angels" (messengers) of the churches (Rev. 1:20), showing that He cares for those churches and their pastors. He's walking among seven golden candlesticks, which we're told in verse 20 represent churches. They represent all of the churches, and through this image, the Lord is trying to give to John and the Church the message that He is walking among them, that He cares about them, and that He loves them. He is not some distant and impersonal God who is aloof and uncaring.

The Assurance

John is so overcome by this wonderful vision of His resurrected and glorified Lord, that he falls at Jesus' feet as if dead (Rev. 1:17). Jesus responds with one of the most comforting statements in all the Word of God: "Do not be afraid; I am the first and the last, and the living One; and I was dead, and behold, I am alive forevermore, and I have the keys of death and of Hades." Jesus is saying, "I am the beginning of history, the end of history, and the meaning of history. I am in control of history. And I have power over life and death."

Jesus' appearance and words are intended to reassure a Church under severe persecution. The hearts of first century Christians, including John's, must have been greatly encouraged, even as Christians today are encouraged by these words.

Chapters 2 and 3

As we move to chapters 2 and 3, the focus shifts from Jesus the glorified One to Jesus the overcomer who is encouraging His Church to persevere and overcome with Him.

The Letters

Chapters 2 and 3 present us with seven letters written by Jesus to seven churches. These are very interesting letters because, first of all, they are letters to seven real churches. But these churches were selected for a reason, and that's because they are representative of all churches existing at that time and today.

Let's just look at the types of churches that are represented in these seven letters. The first church addressed is Ephesus (Rev. 2:1), which was a legalistic church. It was a church that dotted the "i's" and crossed the "t's," but it had lost its love. In verse 8 we are introduced to the church of Smyrna, which is representative of persecuted churches. In verse 12 we have the church of Pergamum, which is the liberal church. It's the church that doesn't care anything about doctrine. It's the opposite of Ephesus. It embraces anyone. Then in verse 18 we have the church of Thyatira, which is the pagan church, the church that is full of cultic practices.

Chapter 3 begins with the church of Sardis which is representative of dead churches. It has a reputation of being alive, but in reality it is dead. The next church mentioned, the church of Philadelphia (Rev. 3:7), is the church that we would all like to be a member of because it is the alive church for which Jesus has no criticism whatsoever. And then, finally, we have in verse 14 the church of Laodicea. In many respects it is the most pathetic of all the churches because it's the worldly and apathetic church — the church that is neither hot nor cold because it just simply could not care less.

The Symbolic Significance

Now, as I said, these seven churches are representatives of every kind of church that exists today. You will find your church in one of these seven or in a combination of them. I think they are also representative of seven different kinds of Christians. So I ask you, are you a legalistic Christian? A persecuted Christian? Liberal? Worldly? Are you dead? Are you alive? Are you apathetic? You will find yourself reflected in one of these letters.

I believe these seven churches are also representative of seven periods of church history. All seven types of churches have always existed, and exist today, but one type has dominated each period of church history.

The Prophetic Significance

The church at Ephesus is representative of the apostolic period from A.D. 30 to 95, when the Church was concerned about organization and doctrine to the point that it became legalistic. The church at Smyrna represents the persecuted church or the martyr church that existed from A.D. 95 to about 312. It's the Church that existed at the time that the Book of Revelation was written. Then we have the liberal church of Pergamum representing the apostate church that existed from 312 to 590. This period developed after the Emperor Constantine was converted and the Church and the state were welded together. As is always the case in such unions, the state began to corrupt the Church.

The church at Thyatira represents the dark, pagan period from 590 to 1517 when the papacy developed and the Church became full of Babylonian occultic practices. When we come to the Reformation in 1517, we think of it as a time of life. But it was only partially so. The Reformation produced the Protestant state churches of Europe — churches that had a reputation for being alive but were really dead because of their union with the state. So the church of Sardis, the dead church with the reputation for being alive, represents the post-Reformation period from 1517 to about 1750.

The opposite of Sardis is the church at Philadelphia, the alive church. It represents the period of church history from about 1750, when the Church began to send missionaries out all over the world, until about 1925, when the German School of Higher Criticism invaded seminaries worldwide and destroyed many people's faith in the Word of God. As a result, people began to look upon the Bible not as the revealed Word of God, but as man's search for God, and therefore they decided it was full of myth, legend, and superstition.

The Contemporary Church

The Church of today is represented by the church of Laodicea, a church that says to the world, "I am rich, and have become wealthy, and have need of nothing." But Jesus says to that church, "You are wretched and miserable and poor and blind and naked" (Rev. 3:17). It is a worldly, apathetic, apostate church that will not even let Jesus in the front door (Rev. 3:20).

The best summary of these letters I have ever encountered is the one penned by John Stott in his book *Basic Christianity*.[2] He sees the message of Jesus as threefold in nature. To a sinful Church, He is saying, "I know of your sin, repent!" To a doubtful Church, He is saying, "I know of your doubt, believe!" To a fearful Church, He is saying, "I know of your fear, endure." Repent, believe, and endure — that's a very relevant message for the Church today.

The Promises

One final thing about these letters. Please note that each of these seven letters end with promises to overcomers. I would exhort you to go through and make a list of them. You will find a total of 13 promises. Look, for example, at Revelation 2:26: "He who overcomes, and he who keeps My deeds until the end, to him I will give authority over the nations; and he shall rule them with a rod of iron." That's just one of the 13 promises. This promise is that the redeemed will rule over the nations of earth. That, of course, is speaking about the millennial reign of Jesus Christ.

There are 12 other marvelous promises. One that I find particularly intriguing is contained in Revelation 2:17, where we are told that every overcomer will receive a white stone with a new name written on it. God loves to change names at critical points in people's lives. When He made His covenant with Abram, He changed his name to Abraham ("father of a multitude"). Abram's wife, Sarai, had her name changed to Sarah ("princess"). Jacob ("supplanter") was changed to Israel ("he who strives with God"). New names were given to Simon and Saul (Peter and Paul) when they were commissioned to serve the Lord (Matt. 16:18 and Acts 13:9).

Believers will be given new names after their resurrection. The white stone represents their innocence before God due to their faith in Jesus. I suspect the new name written on the stone will be related to our spiritual pilgrimage in this life. Wouldn't it be great to be given the name of Faith or Perseverance or Love? Wouldn't it be embarrassing to receive the new name of Wishy-Washy?

All the promises are made to "overcomers." Are you an overcomer? Are you an heir of these 13 wonderful promises? An overcomer is defined in 1 John 5:5 as "he who believes that Jesus is the Son of God." Such a one, John says, "overcomes the world."

Chapter 4

With chapter 4 the focus shifts from the Church to God the Father — as John is suddenly transported "in the Spirit" (Rev. 4:1) from earth to heaven and is ushered into the throne room of God.

The Rapture

I believe John's catching up to heaven is a symbolic type of the Rapture of the Church. Notice verse 1: "After these things," John says, "I looked and behold, a door standing open in heaven, and the first voice which I had heard, like the sound of a trumpet speaking with me, said, 'Come up here, and I will show you what must take place after these things.' "

A door opens in heaven, and John is taken up to heaven from earth. That door opens again in Revelation 19:11 and through it comes Jesus on a white horse returning to earth — and behind Him comes His bride, the Church (Rev. 19:14). The clear implication is that the Church will be in heaven with Jesus during the Tribulation.

In this regard, I think it is significant that the Church, which is the focus of chapters 2 and 3, is not mentioned again by name in the book until Revelation 22:16. There is mention of "saints" (Rev. 13:7, for example), but I believe these are the people who accept Jesus as Lord and Savior during the Tribulation.

The Throne Room

The blessing John was given of seeing the throne room of God is a very special one that few other people have enjoyed. The prophet Micaiah, who lived during the time of King Jehoshaphat, told the king on one occasion, "I saw the Lord sitting on His throne, and all the host of heaven standing by Him on His right and on His left" (1 Kings 22:19). When Isaiah received his call as a prophet, he "saw the Lord, sitting on a throne, lofty and exalted, with the train of His robe filling the temple" (Isa. 6:1). Ezekiel had a similar experience when he was called to be a prophet. He reported seeing a throne that was like a sapphire which was engulfed in a great radiance that looked like a rainbow (Ezek. 1:26–28). Daniel reported seeing God's throne in a night vision (Dan. 7:13–14), and Paul states that he was taken up to heaven where he "heard inexpressible words" (2 Cor. 12:1–4).

What John saw was similar to these previous reports. He sees blazing light emanating from the throne (Rev. 4:5). There is a rainbow encircling the throne, testifying to the faithfulness of God in keeping His promises (Rev. 4:3). He sees seven lamps of fire before the throne (Rev. 4:5) which he says represent the seven-fold nature of the Holy Spirit (Isa. 11:1–2).

He also sees 24 mysterious "elders" sitting before the throne, clothed in white garments with golden crowns on their heads (Rev. 4:4). These are dressed like the redeemed in heaven who are described in Revelation 19:8 as attending the marriage feast of the Lamb. They could very well be representatives of the redeemed, 12 representing the Old Testament saints (perhaps the heads of the 12 tribes of Israel) and 12 representing New Testament saints (perhaps the 12 apostles).

He also sees "four living creatures full of eyes in front and behind" (Rev. 4:6). Each has a different face — one like a lion, another like a calf, the third like a man, and the fourth like an eagle. These are probably the seraphim which Isaiah saw in his vision (Isa. 6:2). These appear to be representative of God's creation, and their role appears to be both guardians of the throne and worship leaders.

Heavenly Worship

Everyone John sees around God's throne appears to be caught up in worshiping the Father. They are singing praises to God. Consider the song recorded in verse 8: "Holy, Holy, Holy is the Lord God, the Almighty, who was and is and who is to come." Notice the three attributes of God that are emphasized in this song — His holiness, His power, and His eternal nature.

The second song John hears emphasizes the power of God. He is extolled as Creator of all things and is therefore declared to be worthy to receive "glory and honor and power" (Rev. 4:11). This emphasis on God's power is designed to encourage the Church during any time it is caught up in suffering and persecution. It is intended to remind the Church that God is on His throne, that He still hears prayers, that He still answers prayers, and that He still performs miracles. In short, God is in control, and He has the wisdom and power to orchestrate all the evil of man and Satan to the triumph of Jesus Christ. What a comforting thought!

Chapter 5

As chapter 5 opens, the focus shifts back to Jesus. He appears as the worthy Lamb.

In the midst of the glorious scene of worship which John describes in chapter 4, he suddenly notices a little scroll in the right hand of God, a scroll that is sealed with seven seals. John is very concerned about that scroll because he knows what it is. It is the title deed of the earth. (This will be made clear when we get to chapter 10.) That title deed is important because this earth was created for man. God gave man dominion over it. But mankind lost that dominion to Satan when Adam and Eve sinned against God. One of the reasons Jesus died on the cross was to restore the earth to the children of God. That's what He meant in the Sermon on the Mount when He said, "The gentle [the meek] shall inherit the earth" (Matt. 5:5). He was quoting a promise made in the Old Testament in Psalm 37. Jesus paid the price on the cross to redeem this promise. It will be fulfilled when He returns.

The Worthy One

So John is concerned about the earth's title deed, especially because no one in heaven seems worthy to open the scroll. But he is suddenly told that his concern is unfounded because there is one who is worthy. He is the "Lion of the tribe of Judah" (Rev. 5:5). John turns to look at the Lion, and what does he see? A little bloody Lamb! (Rev. 5:6). Of course, what he sees is Jesus Christ who is both the Lamb and the Lion. He came the first time as the Lamb to be sacrificed for the sins of the world (Isa. 53:7). He is going to return as the Lion of Judah to pour out the wrath of God upon those who have rejected the grace, mercy and love of God (Jer. 25:30–31).

When Jesus steps up to the throne and takes the scroll, all of heaven breaks forth in a mighty song: "Worthy are You to take the book, and to break its seals; for You were slain, and purchased for God with Your blood men from every tribe and tongue and people and nation. You have made them to be a kingdom and priests to our God; and they will reign upon the earth" (Rev. 5:9–10).

The Future Reign

Notice the promise that the redeemed "will reign upon the earth." Those who deny a future reign of Jesus try to argue that He is reigning now through His saints, the Church. But if that is true, then He is doing a very poor job, because all the nations of the world are in revolt against Him, and the Church is caught up in apostasy.

Furthermore, the Word says that when Jesus reigns, "the earth will be full of the knowledge of the Lord as the waters cover the sea" (Isa. 11:9). No such condition exists today. The heavenly host is clearly singing about a time yet future when the redeemed will reign with Jesus upon the earth.

Again, this is the reiteration of an Old Testament promise found in Daniel 7. In that chapter Daniel tells us that he saw a night vision in which the Son of Man was presented to God the Father and was given dominion over "all the peoples, nations, and men of every language" (Dan. 7:13–14). He then adds that "the saints of the Highest One will receive the kingdom and possess the kingdom forever" (Dan. 7:18). He concludes the chapter by repeating this promise in greater detail: "Then [after the destruction of the Antichrist] the sovereignty, the dominion, and the greatness of all the kingdoms under the whole heaven will be given to the people of the saints of the Highest One" (Dan. 7:27).

Chapter 6

Chapter 6 begins with the Lamb opening the first seal of the little scroll. This action launches the first series of judgments from God's throne — the seal judgments. From this point on to chapter 19, the book is dedicated to describing a seven-year period of time called the Tribulation. Throughout these 13 chapters, Jesus is the wrathful One, pouring out the wrath of God on those who have rejected God's love, grace, and mercy.

The Tribulation

The concept of a time of worldwide tribulation is well established in Old Testament prophecy. It was first mentioned by Moses in Deuteronomy 4:30 when he told the Children of Israel that there would come a time "in the latter days" when they would be placed in great "distress" and would return to the Lord. Jeremiah later referred to it as "the time of Jacob's distress" (Jer. 30:7). Isaiah and Zephaniah, together with John in Revelation, make it clear that the Tribulation will affect all the world (Isa. 24, Zeph. 1, and Rev. 6–18), but — as we shall see — the second half (the final three and a half years) will focus on the nation of Israel. For this reason, Jesus, in speaking to the Jews, referred to the last half of the Tribulation as the "great tribulation," not because it would be a more severe time, but because it would be the time during which the Jews would suffer the most.

This great period of unparalleled horror is often referred to as "Daniel's 70th week." This title refers back to Daniel 9:24–27 where the prophet states that God intends to accomplish six purposes among the Jewish people during a period of 70 weeks of years (490 years). Daniel says the first 69 weeks of years will stretch from the rebuilding of the Temple (following the Babylonian captivity) to the coming of the Messiah. He states this will be followed by the destruction of the Temple once again (Dan. 9:26). He then says that the final week of years will begin when "the prince who is to come" (a reference to the Antichrist) makes a covenant with Israel that will allow them to rebuild their Temple (Dan. 9:27).

The Seal Judgments

As chapter 6 opens, the Tribulation period begins, and we get a foretaste of what it's going to be like — a terrible, terrible period. In verse 2 a rider on a white horse goes forth to conquer. This is the Antichrist riding on a white horse as an imitator of Jesus who will return at the end of the Tribulation, also riding on a white horse (Rev. 19:11). He goes forth to conquer the world. Jesus does not conquer by war. Jesus conquers by the power of the Word of God. So this is definitely the Antichrist.

The result is war, famine, and death. One-fourth of the earth dies in this initial pouring out of the seal judgments (Rev. 6:3–8). That's one and a half billion people in today's terms! Many of those who die are those who are converted to Jesus during this Tribulation period. They are martyred for

Jesus Christ, and so in verses 9 and following we see the spirits of the martyrs in heaven crying out to God, "How long O Lord, holy and true, will You refrain from judging and avenging our blood on those who dwell on the earth?"

A Preview of the End

With the opening of the sixth seal, we come across our first flash-forward to the end of the Tribulation. It's as if God is answering these martyrs by assuring them that He is going to pour out His wrath and that the evil people of this earth will be ultimately destroyed. And so we get a flash-forward to the end of the Tribulation, and we begin to see how terrible that day will be when Jesus returns. The stars fall from the sky; the sky is split apart like a scroll; and the greatest earthquake in all of history occurs. The political leaders of the earth crawl into caves and cry out for the rocks and the mountains to fall upon them because the wrath of the Lamb of God is so great (Rev. 6:13–17).

Chapter 7

Chapter 6 ends with a question: "Who is able to stand" before the wrath of the Lamb? (Rev. 6:17). Chapter 7 begins by answering that question. Before we get to the answer, let me note that chapter 7 is the first of several parenthetical passages. These are passages that interrupt the action in order to insert a word of encouragement to the reader.

Chapter 7 assures the reader that there are two groups — a group of Jews and a group of Gentiles — who will be able to endure the wrath of the Lamb. The first is a group of 144,000 born- again Jewish servants. They are probably going to be converted at the very beginning of the Tribulation by the Lord's supernatural destruction of the Russian army upon the hills of Israel — an event that is described in Ezekiel 38 and 39. It says here in verse 3 that they will be "bond-servants" of God. I think that means they will go forth as messengers of God and will preach the entire period of the Tribulation as God's missionaries to the world.

Salvation During the Tribulation

You see, the purpose of the Tribulation is not primarily punishment. The purpose is to bring people to repentance. God does not wish that any should perish, but that all should be brought to repentance (2 Pet. 3:9).

There is going to be a great harvest of souls during the Tribulation. Some people will undoubtedly come to the Lord in response to the Rapture. Others will repent and accept the Lord in response to the terror of the Tribulation judgments. Others will be brought to the Lord by the preaching of the 144,000. Others will respond to the message of two special witnesses of God that we will read about in chapter 11. And finally in chapter 14 we are told there's going to be an angel who will be sent out to preach the gospel at the end of the Tribulation to every creature on the face of the earth.

Martyrdom During the Tribulation

Most men will reject the gospel, but many will be saved, and most of those will be martyred. So the second group we see in chapter 7, beginning with verse 9, is a great host of people from every nation — all tribes, people, and tongues — standing before the throne and before the Lamb clothed in white robes. John asks who they are, and he is told in verse 14, "These are the ones who come out of the great tribulation, and they have washed their robes and made them white in the blood of the Lamb." I believe these are the ones who are converted by the preaching of the 144,000. They are murdered by the Antichrist and his agents.

Incidentally, this passage in chapter 7 about the great host of Gentile martyrs in heaven answers the often asked question of whether or not there is consciousness after death. This passage makes it clear that there is full consciousness after death. Those who have been martyred are in heaven praising the Lord (Rev. 7:11–12) and serving Him (Rev. 7:15). The souls of the martyrs are pictured as having some sort of intermediate body (Rev. 7:13) — intermediate between their fleshly bodies before death and the glorified bodies they will receive at the time of the resurrection (when Jesus returns at the end of the Tribulation in the second coming).

Chapters 8 and 9

As we come to chapter 8 we're still in the first half of the Tribulation, and God's judgments resume. It says there is silence in heaven for half an hour. It's as if all of heaven is holding its breath before the pouring out of another series of terrible judgments. One wag has said that this period of silence means there won't be any preachers in heaven!

The Trumpet Judgments

In chapter 8 verse 7, the new series of judgments, the trumpet judgments, begin to fall very quickly. They begin with hail and fire mixed with blood being thrown down to the earth (Rev. 8:7). Incredibly, one-third of the earth is burned up and one-third of the earth's waters are polluted (Rev. 8:7–8).

Until recently, most commentators interpreted these trumpet judgments to be supernatural acts of God. They could be. However, when God pours out His wrath, He often does so by relaxing His restraints on human behavior, unleashing people to destroy themselves. This process is clearly outlined in Romans 1:18–32, where we are told that when a society rebels against God and refuses to repent, the Lord will step back, lower His hedge of protection, and allow evil to take its course.

I believe God's restraining hand is the only reason nuclear weapons have not been used since World War II. And speaking of nuclear weapons, I think it is significant that we are the only generation that has ever lived that has the capacity to bring upon ourselves the enormous destruction described in Revelation. This is due to the development of nuclear weapons and intercontinental ballistic missiles. The power of these weapons is breathtaking. For example, one nuclear submarine today carries more fire power than all the bombs dropped during World War II.

Nuclear Devastation

I believe chapter 8 is a first century man's description of a nuclear holocaust. Verse 12 says that one-third of the light of the sun, moon, and stars is blocked out. That is exactly what would happen in a nuclear holocaust because so much debris would be sucked up into the atmosphere by the explosions. The dense cloud that would be produced would cause temperatures to plummet below freezing around the world, causing many people to freeze to death. And that same cloud would be carrying nuclear radiation, which is probably the reason we are told in Revelation 16:2 that by the end of the Tribulation people's bodies will be covered with sores that will not heal. In short, after the nuclear holocaust described in chapter 8, the living will envy the dead.

Jesus himself may have been referring to the age of nuclear weapons when He declared that one of the characteristics of the end times would be "men fainting from fear and the expectation of the things which are coming upon the world; for the powers of the heavens will be shaken" (Luke 21:26).

A Demonic Attack

The trumpet judgments continue in chapter 9 with a plague of demonic locusts. They inflict a sting that causes people to suffer so terribly that they long for death, but they cannot die (Rev. 9:5). Their torment continues for five months (Rev. 9:10). The locusts are empowered to inflict their suffering upon all people except the 144,000 Jews who have been sealed by God (Rev. 9:4).

Hal Lindsey believes this might well be a first century man's description of attack helicopters.[3] It certainly could be that, for the text says the locusts have faces like men (Rev. 9:7), breastplates of iron (Rev. 9:9), and "the sound of their wings was like the sound of . . . many horses rushing to battle" (Rev. 9:9). But John says they are commanded by "the angel of the abyss" called Apollyon (destroyer), and I think that bit of information is an indication that this is a supernatural, demonic plague (Rev. 9:11).

Another Demonic Attack?

When the sixth trumpet is blown (Rev. 9:13), an army of 200 million is let loose. This terrible scourge proceeds to kill one-third of those left alive after the seal judgments. Combined with the one-fourth of humanity that died in the war of the seal judgments, this means one-half of the world's population will be killed in the first half of the Tribulation. That's three billion people in today's terms!

Is this army also demonic in nature? It is hard to tell from the text. It certainly sounds supernatural in nature when it says "the heads of the horses are like the heads of lions; and out of their mouths proceed fire and smoke and brimstone" (Rev. 9:17). But it could very well be that this is a first century man's description of modern day tanks. Also, this army of 200 million could very well be the same one mentioned in Revelation 16:2 that is commanded by the "the kings of the east."

An Asian Revolt

The Book of Daniel states that an army will march against the Antichrist from the east (Dan. 11:44). Daniel says that when the Antichrist hears of this army, the news will greatly disturb him, and he will retreat to a place "between the seas" where he will prepare to confront the army (Dan. 11:44–45). That place, between the Sea of Galilee and the Mediterranean Sea, would be the Valley of Jezreel, or the "Valley of Har-Magedon" (Armageddon), as it is called in Revelation 16:16.

I believe this passage in Daniel indicates that the nations of Asia will revolt against the Antichrist. As they march across Asia, they will slaughter one-third of humanity. When they reach the Euphrates River, it will be dried up to allow them to cross into the Valley of Armageddon where they will attack the armies of the Antichrist (Dan. 11:40–45 and Rev. 16:12, 16). With 200 million Asian troops, together with the massive army of the Antichrist, all assembled for battle in the Valley of Armageddon when Jesus returns, it is no wonder that His supernatural destruction of them, described in Zechariah 14:12, will result in blood running as deep as a horse's bridle for a distance of 200 miles (Rev. 14:20).

Mankind in Rebellion

Chapter 9 ends on a very sad note. We are told that despite the unparalleled carnage of the trumpet judgments, "The rest of mankind, who were not killed by these plagues, did not repent of the works of their hands, so as not to worship demons, and the idols . . . and they did not repent of their murders nor of their sorceries nor of their immorality nor of their thefts" (Rev. 9:20–21).

At this point in the Tribulation, it's as if man is shaking his fist at God. As Billy Graham has often said, "The same sun that melts the butter, hardens the clay." The gospel sometimes melts hearts and sometimes hardens hearts, depending upon whether or not the person is willing to receive the message. The same is true of the judgments of God.

Chapter 10

As we arrive at chapter 10 the chronological action stops once again. This is what I call "the rhythm" of the Book of Revelation. The action builds — the terror mounts — it gets worse and worse, and then, all of a sudden, it comes to a screaming halt, and a parenthetical passage is inserted to assure us that everything is going to work out all right. After all, by the time you get to the end of chapter 9 the world situation looks pretty grim. So, chapter 10 is a parenthesis that presents a flash-forward to assure the reader that everything is going to turn out okay in the end.

An Unusual Angel

John suddenly sees a very unusual angel — a "strong angel." The angel is clothed with a cloud, he has a rainbow upon his head, his face is like the sun, and his feet are like pillars of fire (Rev. 10:1). I don't think there's much doubt who this is. This mighty angel is Jesus. The point is not that Jesus is an angel, because we know from Hebrews chapter 1 and from the rest of the Bible, He is not an angel. He is God in the flesh. He is therefore greater than all the angels, and that's the reason the angels worship Him (Heb. 1:6). He has existed forever, whereas the angels were created. The imagery here is based upon the Old Testament passages that present Jesus in His pre-incarnate state as "the angel of the Lord," which is a term of endearment. (See Exod. 3:2–6.)

We know this is Jesus because He is clothed with a cloud which is a representation of the Shekinah glory of God. Further, He has a rainbow upon His head, and we saw in chapter 4 that's the symbol of faithfulness that crowns the throne of God. His face is like the sun. That's right out of the description of Jesus in chapter 1 (verse 16), as is the reference to His feet being like pillars of fire (Rev. 1:15).

The clue that clinches the angel's identity is in verse 2 where we are told that He has a little scroll in His right hand which He holds up as He claims possession of the earth. In chapter 5 we learned that Jesus was the only one in all the universe who was qualified to take that scroll from the hand of God the Father. What we have here is another flash-forward to the end of the Tribulation to assure us that everything is going to turn out all right. Jesus is going to return in triumph to claim the earth for the children of God.

Chapter 11

In chapter 11 the Tribulation action resumes. John is told to measure the temple of God. This is a reference to the Tribulation temple which will be an apostate institution since it will house a reinstituted Mosaic sacrificial worship system. The order to measure it with a rod is symbolic of its being measured for God's judgment.

Tribulation Preachers

In verse 3 we are introduced to two witnesses of God. No one knows for sure who these are, but based upon the miracles they perform, they could be Elijah and Moses. I think it is more likely that they will be Elijah and Enoch. I say that because they are the only two men that were raptured to heaven and thus did not experience death. Further, they are representatives of all of mankind, for Elijah prophesied to the Jews whereas Enoch was a prophet to the Gentiles.

Whoever they may be, they will preach the Word with great power during the first half of the Tribulation. Then, in the middle of the Tribulation when the Antichrist reveals himself, he will kill these two great witnesses, and their bodies will lie in the streets of Jerusalem for three and a half days as the whole earth rejoices (Rev. 11:9). Think of it — the earth will be so evil that people will rejoice over the death of these right-eous men (Rev. 11:10). Then, after three and a half days, they will suddenly be resurrected and caught up to heaven before the eyes of all mankind as the world watches on television (Rev. 11:11–12). At that point, God shakes Jerusalem with a terrible earthquake in retribution, and some of the inhabitants are so terrified that they turn their hearts to God (Rev. 11:13).

Chapter 12

We come now to chapter 12, one of the most crucial chapters in the book because it explains what Revelation is all about.

The first six verses of Chapter 12 constitute another parenthetical passage. But unlike the previous ones we have run across, this one is a flashback rather than a flash-forward. It is designed to help us better understand what the Tribulation is all about.

What the chapter in effect says is that the Tribulation is the consummation of a cosmic battle between God and Satan that has been going on in the supernatural world since the revolt of man in the Garden of Eden. It reminds us that Satan tried to stop the first coming of the Messiah, just as he is now trying to prevent His second coming. The chapter is full of symbols. Let's take a look at them.

Meaningful Symbols

The first symbol in chapter 12 is "a woman clothed with the sun," with the moon under her feet, and a crown of twelve stars on her head (Rev. 12:1). Many different interpretations have been given of this imagery. Some commentators claim that this woman represents the Church. Catholics claim she is Mary, the mother of Jesus.

Here is a classic example of why it is important to let the Bible interpret itself, wherever possible. The point is that this imagery comes right out of Joseph's dream in Genesis 37, where the sun stood for Jacob, the moon for Rachel, and the stars for Joseph's brothers (Gen. 37:9–11). So, we can conclude that this woman represents the nation of Israel, the descendants of Jacob.

The woman is pregnant and is about to give birth. This refers to Israel providing the Messiah to the world. In verse 3 "a great red dragon," which is Satan, tries to devour "a male child" when He is born — which, of course, is exactly what Satan tried to do when he motivated King Herod to send his army to Bethlehem to kill all the babies at the time of Jesus' birth. But the male child, Jesus, is "caught up to God and to His throne" (the Ascension) where He waits "to rule all the nations with a rod of iron" (Rev. 12:5).

These verses remind us that there is a great cosmic struggle going on over the dominion of planet Earth. God originally gave that dominion to man (Gen. 1:28), but it was stolen by Satan when Adam and Eve gave in to his temptation and rebelled against God. Consequently, Satan is now "the ruler of this world" (John 12:31) and "the whole world lies in the power of the evil one" (1 John 5:19).

But one of the reasons Jesus died on the cross was to make it possible for man to reassert his rightful dominion over the earth. This is one of the many delayed benefits of the Cross (our glorified bodies being another one). Jesus will reclaim dominion over the earth when He returns at the end of the Tribulation. We saw Him doing that in the flash-forward about the "strong angel" in chapter 10. In chapter 5 verse 13 we are told that the heavenly hosts sing about that glorious day: "To Him who sits on the throne, and to the Lamb, be blessing and honor and glory and *dominion* forever and ever" (emphasis added).

Heavenly War

In verse 7 of chapter 12 the action resumes once again. We are in the middle of the Tribulation, and Satan tries one last time to take the throne of God. The result is a war in heaven (Rev. 12:7). The archangel Michael and the angels under his command fight against Satan and his demonic angels. Satan loses the battle and is cast down to earth (Rev. 12:9). His access to heaven is cut off (Rev. 12:10).

Verse 12 tells us something remarkable. It says that Satan realizes at this point that his time is short. That means Satan knows Bible prophecy! But despite his knowledge, he continues to struggle because he has deceived himself into believing that he can obstruct God's plans and emerge victorious.

Satan on Earth

At this point it appears that Satan actually possesses the Antichrist, even as he possessed Judas (Luke 22:3). We are told in Revelation 13:2 that Satan gives the Antichrist "his power and his throne and great authority." Daniel also says that the Antichrist's power will be mighty, "but not by his own power" (Dan. 8:24).

The first thing Satan does is to motivate the Antichrist to launch a great persecution of "the woman who gave birth to the male child" (Rev. 12:13). In other words, he picks up where Hitler left off with a maniacal campaign to destroy the Jewish people.

According to Daniel, the Antichrist will launch this holocaust by marching into the rebuilt temple in Jerusalem and stopping the sacrifices (Dan. 9:27). He will set up an "abomination of desolation," probably a statue of himself (Matt. 24:15). And he will blaspheme God (Dan. 11:36) and declare himself to be God (2 Thess. 2:4).

The Jews, of course, will be horrified by these actions, and they will revolt. This will prompt the Antichrist to launch an all-out attack on the Jews worldwide. His purpose will be to annihilate every last one of them so that God cannot keep

His promise to save a great remnant at the end of the Tribulation (Zech. 12:10, 13:1 and Rom. 9:27, 11:25–26).

Satan's Anti-Semitism

Keep in mind that Satan hates the Jews with a passion. He hates them because they gave the world the Bible and the Messiah. He also hates them because they are God's Chosen People — chosen to be a witness of what it means to have a relationship with God. Another reason he hates them is because God has promised to save a great remnant of the Jews at the end of the Tribulation, and Satan does not want to see God fulfill that promise.

The Antichrist's extermination campaign in the middle of the Tribulation prompts many Jews to flee "into the wilderness" to a special place where they will be protected and nourished by God for "a time and times and half a time" — a Jewish colloquialism for three and a half years (Rev. 12:14). Daniel indicates the location of the wilderness safe place where the Jews will flee. He states that the Antichrist will conquer all the Middle East except Edom, Moab, and Ammon (Dan. 11:41). These areas are all included in modern-day Jordan.

This wilderness hideaway in Jordan is likely to be the remarkable box canyon city of Petra. It is a city whose buildings are carved out of the walls of the surrounding canyon. In its heyday (4th to 2nd century B.C.), it contained a population of tens of thousands.

Chapter 12 concludes by telling us that Satan is so enraged by God's protection of the Jewish remnant that he decides to "make war with the rest of her offspring, who keep the commandments of God and hold to the testimony of Jesus" — a reference to Messianic Jews and Gentile Christians (Rev. 12:17).

Chapter 13

Chapter 13 tells us how Satan will go about persecuting believers. His agent is the Antichrist who is introduced to us as "a beast" who "comes up out of the sea" (Rev. 13:1). That latter phrase is a symbolic reference to the Gentile nations

(Rev. 17:3), indicating the Antichrist will be a Gentile. Daniel also infers the Antichrist will be a Gentile when he says that he will come from the people who will destroy the temple (Dan. 9:26). The temple was destroyed by the Romans, so the Antichrist must be a person of Roman descent.

Two Beasts

The beast is empowered by Satan (Rev. 13:2), and he immediately begins to blaspheme God (Rev. 13:6), just as Daniel prophesies that he will (Dan. 11:36). Satan also gives him his authority (Rev. 11:2). The beast proceeds to use his power and authority to "make war with the saints." In the process, dominion is granted to him "over every tribe and people and tongue and nation" (Rev. 13:7). In other words, he becomes history's first true worldwide dictator. He very quickly accomplishes something that Alexander the Great, Napoleon, and Hitler dreamed of and died trying to achieve. Even more important, from Satan's viewpoint, the Antichrist becomes the object of worldwide worship (Rev. 13:8).

At this point (Rev. 13:11) we are introduced to another "beast" who rises up "out of the earth" (literally, "the land"). Just as the sea is a prophetic symbol for the Gentile nations, the land is a symbol of Israel. Thus, the implication here is that this second beast will be a Jew. This beast is later referred to as "the false prophet" (Rev. 19:20).

The False Prophet

This nefarious character serves as the Antichrist's right-hand man. He exercises the authority of the Antichrist (Rev. 13:12) in carrying out both political and religious duties.

Spiritually, the false prophet serves as the head of a one-world religion, seeing to it that everyone worships the Antichrist (Rev. 13:12). He will dazzle and deceive people with great signs, including giving life to a statue of the Antichrist (Rev. 13:14–15). His demonic religious system will consist of people drawn from all the world's religions. The false prophet will argue in the name of tolerance that there are many roads to God — that God has revealed himself in religions like Islam, Judaism, Christianity, Buddhism, Hinduism, Animism, and the New Age movement, to name only a few. He will tell people they can pray to whatever god they please as long as they accept the Antichrist as the messiah of their god.

Politically, the false prophet is the one responsible for administering the Antichrist's enforcement system (Rev. 13:16). It is based on the requirement for all of mankind to take the name or the number of the beast, which is 666. No one can buy and no one can sell without the mark or the name of the beast on their right hand or their forehead (Rev. 13:16–17). And since no faithful Christian or observant Jew will take this mark, at this point all Christians and Jews will become outlaws. They will have to hide out in the countryside and live off the land. They will be hunted down like animals, and most of them will be killed — not all, but most. It will be a horrible period of unparalleled persecution of believers in the true God.

A Satanic Trinity

As we move into the second half of the Tribulation, the earth is cursed with the presence of a satanic trinity. The false god is Satan who has been cast down to earth and cut off from heaven. The false messiah is the Antichrist who demands the world's worship. The false counterpart of the Holy Spirit is the false prophet whose responsibility is to persuade people to give their allegiance to the Antichrist.

It is no wonder that the earth will "reel to and fro like a drunkard" and "totter like a shack" (Isa. 24:20). This satanic trio will cause so much havoc that "the earth will be completely laid waste and completely despoiled" (Isa. 24:3). Jesus emphasized the horrendous nature of this period by stating that if it were not cut short by the Lord, no one would be left alive (Matt. 24:22).

Chapter 14

Because the situation is so terrible at the end of chapter 13, chapter 14 presents another parenthetical pause designed to encourage the reader. What happens in this chapter is that we are given another flash-forward to the end of the Tribulation to assure us that we are going to be victorious in the end.

We are first given a glimpse of Jesus the Lamb standing on Mt. Zion in Jerusalem (Rev. 14:1). With Him are the 144,000 faithful Jewish servants. This scene is given to assure us that at the end of the Tribulation Jesus is going to return to the earth in triumph, and all the 144,000 Jews will be protected to the end.

A Procession of Angels

The remainder of chapter 14 presents a panoramic preview of what is going to happen during the rest of the Tribulation. We are told that an angel will go forth and preach the gospel to every person on the face of the earth (Rev. 14:6). Isn't that amazing? God is so good! Even while men are shaking their fists at Him, the Lord, in His patience and long-suffering and kindness and mercy sends forth an angel to preach the gospel to every creature on the face of the earth before He pours out His final wrath. Do you remember what Jesus said in Matthew 24? He said that "the gospel of the kingdom shall be preached in the whole world for a witness to all the nations, and then the end shall come" (Matt. 24:14). Well, this is the fulfillment of that prophecy right at the end of the Tribulation.

A second angel is sent forth to proclaim that Babylon, the end-time empire of the Antichrist, will be destroyed (Rev. 14:8). The implication of this warning is for everyone to come out of Babylon, a message that is made clear in chapter 18 verse 4 where a voice from heaven proclaims, "Come out of her [Babylon], my people, so that you will not participate in her sins and receive her plagues." A third angel is then sent out to warn people that they are not to worship the Antichrist or receive his mark, because if they do, they will suffer the wrath of God (Rev. 14:9–10).

The chapter concludes with another preview of the second coming of Jesus (Rev. 14:14–20). As He comes on the clouds, He swings His sickle and reaps the earth, separating the chaff from the good wheat. Sinners are cast into "the great wine press of the wrath of God" (Rev. 14:19).

Chapters 15 and 16

Having been reassured that Jesus and His saints will triumph, we are now ready to proceed with the final pouring out of God's wrath. Chapter 15 introduces us to this final stage of the Tribulation, stating that with the last series of judgments, "the wrath of God is *finished*" (Rev. 15:1, emphasis added). This statement is a clear indication that the entire Tribulation is a period of the pouring out of God's wrath. And what are we told in Romans 5:9? We are told that those of us who are redeemed are guaranteed protection from the wrath of God. Similarly, in 1 Thessalonians 1:10 we are told that Jesus is coming to save us from the wrath of God. These are indications that we — the Church — are going to be taken out of this world before the Tribulation begins.

The Last Song

As the final wrath of God is about to be poured out in a series of judgments called the bowl judgments, chapter 15 pictures a great number of victorious saints standing before God's throne singing. This is the Bible's last song (Rev. 15:3–4):

> Great and marvelous are Your works, O Lord God, the Almighty; Righteous and true are Your ways, King of the nations! Who will not fear, O Lord, and glorify Your name? For You alone are holy; For all the nations will come and worship before You, For Your righteous acts have been revealed.

What a song! It affirms the power, holiness, and righteousness of God. It assures us that the Lord's dominion over the earth will be reclaimed, and all the nations will be subjected to Him. It is a majestic musical prelude to the final pouring out of God's wrath.

The Bowl Judgments

That final wrath falls in chapter 16. The bowl judgments of God's wrath are poured out in rapid succession. It probably takes no more than a month's time for all of these judgments to occur. Notice that the first judgment results in "loathsome and malignant sores" (Rev. 16:2). These, of course, could be a result of radiation from the previous nuclear war. The second and third bowls of judgment pollute all the water on the planet, both sea water and fresh water (Rev. 16:3–4). And then, just as there's no longer any decent water to drink, a horrible thing happens. The fourth judgment results in the sun being multiplied in its power, and people are scorched with heat (Rev. 16:8–9). You can imagine the suffering and agony this would produce.

The fifth bowl of judgment produces a thick darkness in the area of the Antichrist's throne, which, of course, would be Europe (Rev. 16:10). The sixth bowl dries up the Euphrates River and enables a great army from the east to march into the Valley of Armageddon (Rev. 16:12).

Continuing Rebellion

The rest of the chapter provides a detailed description of the destruction of the Antichrist's kingdom (Rev. 16:17–21). It is a flash-forward to the end of the Tribulation when the great earthquake (already described in Rev. 6:12–17) occurs. The Antichrist's capital city is destroyed (Rev. 16:19) as people are pummeled with "huge hailstones" that weigh 100 pounds each (Rev. 16:21).

The tragedy is that, once again, we are told that most people refuse to repent. Their hearts have become so hardened that they focus their energy on blaspheming God (Rev. 16:11, 21).

Chapter 17

Chapter 17 introduces us to a vile scene of a "great harlot" riding "a scarlet beast" (Rev. 17:1, 3). Women are often used in the Scriptures to symbolize religious systems, and that is the case here. This harlot represents the apostate and corrupt Roman Catholic Church which will dominate the religious scene during the first half of the Tribulation. The church will rally apostate Protestants and practitioners of other religions to rally behind the Antichrist. She is described as being "drunk with the blood of the saints" and with "the blood of the witnesses of Jesus" (Rev. 17:6) because she will persecute all true believers who refuse to cooperate with her, even as she has done historically.

Catholic Apostasy

The apostasy of the Roman Catholic Church has accelerated in recent years in preparation for its role during the first half of the Tribulation. In October 1986, Pope John Paul II invited the leaders of the world's religions to come to Assisi, Italy, to join him in praying for world peace.[4] One hundred sixty representatives came, including the Dali Lama (who considers himself to be a god). Each representative prayed to his own god at the pope's request!

Did the pope believe their gods were real? Or did he believe that they were all praying to the same god, but under different names?

In December 2000 Pope John Paul muddied the waters further when he addressed 30,000 pilgrims in St. Peter's Square. He told the multitude "that all who live a just life will be saved even if they do not believe in Jesus Christ and the Roman Catholic Church."[5] The pope added, "The gospel teaches us that those who live in accordance with the Beatitudes . . . will enter God's kingdom." He concluded by observing that all that is needed for salvation is "a sincere heart."

The Church's Destruction

Notice that the harlot is portrayed as riding on the back of the Antichrist (Rev. 17:3). This symbolism indicates that the church has become a nuisance. The Antichrist has used her to help consolidate his world kingdom, but now she has become enamored with power, and so the Antichrist turns on her and destroys her (Rev. 17:16). He replaces her with his new one-world religion that is headed up by the false prophet.

Chapter 18

Chapter 18 depicts the destruction of the political, economic, and social systems of the Antichrist's kingdom.

Babylon's Destruction

The destruction is swift and total, occurring in one hour of one day (Rev. 18:10). But again, before the destruction falls, God in His tender mercy sends another angel to warn. The angel announces the impending doom of the kingdom (Rev. 18:2) and then implores people to "Come out!" (Rev. 18:4). We are told that the sins of the kingdom "have piled up as high as heaven," and God is ready to remember her iniquities (Rev. 18:5).

As the Antichrist's capital city and kingdom are quickly destroyed by God with pestilence, famine, and fire (Rev. 18:8), the political leaders, merchants, and cargo handlers of the world weep and mourn in despair because of the wealth that is laid to waste (Rev. 18:9, 11, 17, 19).

Where's America?

Many commentators argue that the Babylon of chapter 18 is the United States of America. This view has become particularly popular since the fall of the Soviet Union because it left the United States as the world's only superpower. I do not believe this interpretation can be sustained. The focus of chapter 18 is clearly on the kingdom of the Antichrist, and the prophet Daniel makes it clear that the Antichrist's kingdom will be centered in Europe, representing a resurrection of the old Roman Empire.

Further, it should be kept in mind that although the United States is currently the only superpower, that status is quickly fading as the European Union consolidates. Also, it should be noted that when the Rapture occurs, the United States will be devastated — more so than any other nation. That's because we have more born-again Christians in positions of power (both political and economic) than any other nation in the world. In other words, the United States will not be a superpower when the end of the Tribulation is reached.

Chapter 19

The scene in heaven is radically different from the one on earth at the end of the Tribulation. While all hell is breaking loose on earth and people are weeping and wailing in agony, all of heaven is rejoicing!

Heavenly Hallelujahs

All the heavenly host is shouting "Hallelujah!" as chapter 19 begins. It's the only time this Old Testament term of praise is recorded in the New Testament. And the hallelujahs continue for the first six verses of chapter 19.

Why is everyone in heaven rejoicing? There are several reasons. Verse 2 tells us that they are rejoicing because God has avenged the blood of Christian martyrs by destroying the Antichrist's kingdom. The second reason they are shouting "Hallelujah!" is because the judgment of the saints has been completed, and they are about to celebrate their union with Jesus — as the bride of Christ — at the greatest banquet the cosmos has ever experienced. Notice carefully how the Bride is dressed: "The marriage of the Lamb has come and His bride has made herself ready. It was given to her to clothe herself in fine linen, bright and clean" (Rev. 19:7–8). The third reason they are celebrating is because the time has come for Jesus to return to earth in glory and power.

The Second Coming

The description of the Lord's return begins in verse 11, immediately following the celebration of the marriage feast of the Lamb in heaven. John sees heaven open, and out comes Jesus riding on a white horse. He does not return alone. Look at verse 14: "And the armies which are in heaven, clothed in fine linen, white and clean, were following Him on white horses." These are not angels. These are the very same people described earlier in verse 8. They are the bride of Christ, His church. This is one of the strongest evidences for a pre-Tribulation Rapture, for the Church is clearly depicted here as being in heaven with Jesus at the end of the Tribulation, and the Church returns with Him.

Jesus is portrayed returning as "the Kings of kings, and Lord of lords" (Rev. 19:16). Right now He is not a king. Right now He is our high priest in heaven, our mediator before the throne of God (Heb. 8:1). But when He returns, He is coming in power and glory as the King of kings and the Lord of lords. His initial purpose is spelled out in verse 11 where we are told that He is coming to "judge and wage war" against the enemies of God. Verse 15 says that He is going to "strike down the nations" with the word of His mouth, and He is going to rule over them with a "rod of iron" (Rev. 19:15).

The Defeat of the Antichrist

Chapter 19 concludes with what people often refer to as the "Battle of Armageddon." Verses 17–21 describe the Lord's defeat of the Antichrist and his forces which, according to Daniel 11and Revelation 16, are camped in the Valley of Armageddon. But there really is no battle. Jesus does not send forth an army to fight. Zechariah 14:12 makes it clear that the Lord simply speaks a word which results in the Antichrist and his forces being instantly destroyed by a supernatural plague. Paul affirms this in 2 Thessalonians 2:8 where he states that the Antichrist will be slain by the Lord "with the breath of His mouth."

Zechariah adds that the eyeballs of the soldiers will melt in their sockets, their tongues will melt in their mouths and their skin will drop from their bodies (Zech. 14:12). All that will remain will be their bones and blood, which will be as deep as a horse's bridle for a distance of 200 miles! (Rev. 14:20).

This terrible carnage is called "the supper of God" (Rev. 19:17). What a contrast we have here between the beautiful marriage feast in heaven and the ghastly supper of God on earth when the army of the Antichrist will become food for the vultures. And the crucial question is which of those feasts are you going to attend? Are you going to be invited to the glorious wedding feast in Heaven, or are you going to be feasted upon by the vultures at the supper of God here on earth? At one feast you are the honored guest; at the other, you are the meal! The choice is yours. Your fate depends entirely on whether or not you put your faith in Jesus as Lord and Savior (1 John 5:5).

Chapter 20

As chapter 20 opens, Jesus is ready to begin His reign here on earth. But there's one last piece of business He has to take care of. He has dealt with the Antichrist and the false prophet. He's defeated them and their armies, and He has thrown them into "the lake of fire" — which is hell — where they will be tormented forever and ever (Rev. 19:20 and 20:10). But there's still one last rebel left, and that's Satan. So, the Lord's first business in chapter 20 is to bind Satan and put him into a great abyss were he will be confined for the next thousand years (Rev. 20:1–3). During that time Satan and his demonic hoards will not be allowed to roam upon the earth.

Reigning with Jesus

Then chapter 20 says that we — the redeemed — are going to reign with the Lord Jesus Christ for a thousand years (Rev. 20:4). That reign is not described here in great detail. You will find the detailed description of it in the Old Testament, particularly in the book of Isaiah. We are told that Jesus will rule with "a rod of iron" (Rev. 3:27, 12:5, 19:15 and Ps. 2:9), and we are told that some people will reign with Him — specifically, those to whom judgment has been given (Rev. 20:4).

Who, specifically, will reign with Jesus? According to Daniel 7, Old Testament saints will be included in this group: "The saints of the Highest One will receive the kingdom. . . . Then the sovereignty, the dominion, and the greatest of all the kingdoms under the whole heaven will be given to the people of the saints of the Highest One" (verses 18 and 27). The apostles will also be included. In Matthew 19:28 Jesus promised His apostles that "in the regeneration when the Son of Man will sit on His glorious throne, you shall sit upon twelve thrones, judging the twelve tribes of Israel." Those of us who have become saints during the Church Age will certainly be included. That promise is made in several places in the New Testament (2 Tim. 2:12, Rev. 2:26–27, 3:21, and 5:9–10). Finally, the Tribulation martyrs who die for Jesus will be included (Rev. 20:4).

What will we do? Some of us will be administrators, serving as mayors, governors, and kings. Jesus made the point in one of His parables that degrees of reigning authority would be part of the rewards that believers would receive, based upon their faithfulness in this life (Luke 19:11–27). Others of us will serve as judges. Most of us will serve as teachers — that's right, we're going to provide the worldwide educational system, serving as "shepherds" and "priests of God" (Jer. 3:15 and Rev. 20:6). It will be our responsibility to bring each person born during the Millennium to salvation through a saving faith in Jesus.

None of us will be legislators because no abomination like the Texas legislature or the United States Congress will exist. The government of the world will be a theocracy in which Jesus will be both the spiritual and governmental leader. The offices of priest and king will be combined in Him (Zech. 6:12–13). He will give the law, and we will teach it and enforce it (Isa. 2:1–4).

The Millennial Population

Who will the redeemed be ruling over? Where will the millennial population come from? The people who will be allowed to go into the Millennium in the flesh will be the small number of Jews and Gentiles who live to the end of the Tribulation who have accepted Jesus Christ as their Lord and Savior. When Jesus returns, we're told that He will judge immediately all those left alive. The Jewish judgment is described in Ezekiel 20:34–38; the Gentile, in Matthew 25:31–46. Those who have not accepted Jesus as Lord and Savior will be consigned to death (Luke 17:34–37).

You and I — the redeemed — will be in glorified bodies, like the body Jesus has now. Just as He mingled and interacted with His disciples after His resurrection while He was in a glorified body and they were in fleshly bodies, in like manner, we who will be in glorified bodies will live among and rule over those who are in fleshly bodies.

Jesus will reign in His glorified body as the King of the world from Jerusalem. We're told in the Old Testament that David in his glorified body will rule as the king of Israel (Ezek. 34:24). And as I said before, some of us will be administrators and some judges, but most of us will be teachers. We will be scattered all over the earth reigning over those in the flesh.

We're told in the Book of Isaiah that life spans will be returned to what they were after the fall in the Garden of Eden — that is, 1,000 years (Isa. 65:17–20). That means the people who enter the Millennium in the flesh, and the children born to them during the Millennium, will live the entire time. Because death will be curtailed and life spans will be extended, the earth will experience a great population explosion. Most likely, by the end of the Millennium, there will be more people on the face of the earth than ever before in the history of mankind. And it will be the responsibility of the redeemed to bring those born during that time to salvation in Jesus Christ.

The Nature of Man

You may think, *Well, of course they will accept Jesus. After all, they will be able to see Him in His glorified body. And they will experience first hand the blessings of His rule*. But remember, Jesus was here before, and all He did was love people and heal them and feed them — and they responded by nailing Him to a cross. The heart of man is going to be no different during this millennial period. Sin will be less because Satan and his demonic hoards will be restrained, but there still will be sin and rebellion in people's hearts because we are born with a sin nature (Jer. 17:9). The evil that is in the world comes from *within* man (Mark 7:20–23). All Satan does is multiply it through temptation.

In fact, that's one of the purposes of the Millennium. God is going to use the Millennium to prove that Satan's religion, Humanism, is wrong when it says that the way to change the world is to change society. Humanists take that position because they believe that evil is rooted in society. But the Word of God says that evil is rooted in the fallen nature of man and that the only way to change the world is to change people's hearts. So God is going to put mankind in a perfect environment for a thousand years, and at the end of that time He's going to let Satan loose. Satan will then expose the seed of rebellion that is in people's hearts. He will do this by convincing the nations to rebel against Jesus (Rev. 20:7–10).

At this point you are probably wondering, "Why would people rebel after experiencing one thousand years of peace, righteousness, and justice?" Well, think for a moment what it would be like to live under "the rule of the rod of iron" in the flesh. The flesh would want all the pleasures of the world — drugs, gambling, illicit sex, and pornography. But these things would not be allowed under Jesus' rule of the rod of iron. Any attempt to indulge the flesh would be met with swift and sure justice. Violators would be tried before judges in glorified bodies, and there would be no appeal, because the judge's decision would be perfect. And so people on the surface will say, "We praise you Jesus!" But there will be seething rebellion in their hearts.

The Last Revolt

Satan is going to expose that rebellious spirit. We're told in Revelation 20:7 that Satan will be let loose to test mankind, and he will rally the nations of the earth against Jesus. This will be man's last revolt against God, and through it God will prove conclusively that you do not change people by simply changing their environment. It is their hearts that must be changed, and that can be done only through the power of the Holy Spirit.

The Tribulation will conclude with God pouring out His wrath on Satan and those who follow him (Rev. 20:9). Satan will be thrown into the lake of fire to join the Antichrist and the false prophet (Rev. 20:10). Then, God will resurrect and judge all the unrighteous who have ever lived — whether in Old Testament times, the Church Age, or the Millennium. This judgment is called "the great white throne judgment" (Rev. 20:11–15). It is the judgment of the damned. All those who ever lived and died outside a faith relationship with God will be judged of their works to determine their eternal destiny. And since no man can be justified before God by his works, all those who come before the Great White Throne will be condemned to "the lake of fire" to experience the "second death" (Rev. 20:14).

Chapter 21

Chapter 21 introduces us to a vision of the eternal state — something we're not told a lot about. But what we're told here is very interesting.

A New Earth

John says, "I saw a new heaven and a new earth" (Rev. 21:1). What happens is that God burns up the old earth. We're told in 2 Peter 3 that He will burn away all the pollution of Satan's last revolt. He will take this earth and reshape it like a hot ball of wax, and out of that fiery inferno will come the new heavens and the new earth, an earth that will be refreshed and beautified and perfected to what God originally created before it was polluted by sin and changed by the curse (2 Pet. 3:10–13). It will probably be greatly enlarged because it is going to serve as the foundation for a gigantic city — the New Jerusalem.

Just think of it! As God creates that new earth, we will most likely be suspended in the heavens inside the New Jerusalem watching the greatest fireworks display in the history of the cosmos. And when it's all over, and the earth is refreshed and renewed, then the Lord will lower us down to the new earth inside the New Jerusalem (Rev. 21:2). We are going to live eternally inside that glorious city located on the new earth.

That's right, the Bible never teaches that we will spend eternity in heaven. It teaches that we will spend eternity in new bodies in a New Jerusalem on a new earth, and it further teaches that God will come down to that new earth and live among us: "I heard a loud voice from the throne, saying, 'Behold, the tabernacle of God is among men, and He shall dwell among them, and they shall be His people, and God Himself shall be among them'" (Rev. 21:3). He's going to wipe away every tear from our eyes, and there will no longer be any suffering — no pain, no death, no sorrow (Rev. 21:4). He is going to make all things new, and we are going to live in perfect bliss in the New Jerusalem (Rev. 21:5).

A New City

The rest of chapter 21 describes the incredible New Jerusalem that Jesus is preparing now (John 14:2). It will be shaped like a cube, 1,500 miles in every direction. It will be a city of incredible beauty, made of pearls and precious stones and gold. There will be no temple in the city because it says that "the Lord God, the Almighty, and the Lamb" will be its temple (Rev. 21:22). God the Father and His Son will live in the city with the redeemed, and the Shekinah glory of God will illumine the city (Rev. 21:23).

A Mystery

One of the great mysteries of Bible prophecy is introduced in Revelation 21:24 where it states that "the nations shall walk by its light [the light emanating from the Shekinah glory in the city], and the kings of the earth shall bring their glory into it." Who are these nations and kings outside the city on the new earth? They must be in fleshly bodies, for we are told in chapter 22 that the leaves of the tree of life inside the city will be used "for the healing of the nations" (Rev. 22:2).

We, the redeemed, are assured that we will reign with Jesus "forever" (Rev. 1:6, 11:15, and 22:5). In order to reign, there must be someone to reign over. We know who that will be during the Millennium. But who are these people on the new earth in the eternal state? Are they people who accepted Jesus during the Millennium? I ask that because we are never told what will become of those who receive Jesus during His millennial reign.

Chapter 22

In chapter 22 we move inside the New Jerusalem. We are told that "a river of the water of life" will flow from the throne of God (Rev. 22:1). This river is most likely a symbolic manifestation of the Holy Spirit. This river will run down the middle of the city's main street, and the tree of life that was in the Garden of Eden will grow on each side of the river, "bearing twelve kinds of fruit, yielding its fruit every month" (Rev. 22:2). There will no longer be any curse, for when God recreates the earth, the curse will be abolished (Rev. 22:3). All of creation will be restored to the perfection that God intended when He created the original earth.

Fellowship and Service

And so we get a glimpse of that great eternal state where we will live eternally with God in new bodies in the New Jerusalem on the new earth. It's only a glimpse, but it's enough to make us yearn for the glory that is to come, particularly when you consider what is said in chapter 22, verse 4. That verse says *we shall see God's face*. The Bible tells us that no one has ever seen the face of God (Exod. 33:20). But one day we, the redeemed, will see His face! That means we are going to have intimate, personal, eternal fellowship with our Creator.

We are also going to serve the Lord eternally (Rev. 22:3). The Bible does not get specific as to the nature of that service, but I know it will be meaningful and fulfilling. I can imagine, for example, that He will magnify and perfect our gifts. Vocalists will sing as they have never sung before, artists will paint with a majesty they never thought possible. And all will be done for the glory and honor of our Creator.

A Call to Prepare

In verse 6 of chapter 22 the focus shifts suddenly from the eternal state to the promise that Jesus will return again.

Jesus states, "I am coming quickly," and then He adds, "Blessed is he who heeds the words of the prophecy of this book." Notice, He says not only the one who hears the words, but the one who *heeds* them.

He then begins to tell us some things that we're to do as we wait for His return. As I outline these for you, ask yourself, "Am I doing these things?" In verse 9 we are told to worship God. In verse 10 we are told "not to seal up the words of the prophecy." That means we are to share it with as many people as possible. Verse 17 exhorts us to yearn daily for the Lord's return. And verse 18 commands us to protect the integrity of God's Word by not allowing anyone to add to it or take away from it.

A Reminder of Judgment

In verse 12 Jesus repeats the wonderful promise that summarizes the book's whole theme. He says, "Behold I am coming quickly." He then adds a warning. He says He will reward every man "according to what he has done." Jesus is coming back, and when He returns there is going to be a judgment of works for both believers and unbelievers. But it will not be for the purpose of determining their eternal destinies. That is determined in this life by whether or not we place our faith in Jesus as Lord and Savior. Believers will be judged at the time of the Rapture to determine their degrees of rewards. Unbelievers will be judged at the end of the Millennium, at the Great White Throne Judgment, to determine their degrees of punishment.

Yes, there are going to be degrees of rewards for believers, both during the Millennium and during eternity. Jesus said we would have various degrees of reigning authority during the Millennium. And the Bible says that special rewards are going to be given to soul winners (Phil. 4:11), martyrs (Rev. 2:10), elders (1 Pet. 5:4), those who exercise self-control (1 Cor. 9:25), and those who live looking for the coming of Jesus (2 Tim. 4:7–8).

The Lord's Last Words

The final words of Jesus spoken on this earth are recorded in Revelation 2:20. He says to John, "Yes, I am coming quickly."

Jesus left us with a glorious promise — a promise to return soon. And notice John's response. He cried out from the depth of his heart, "Amen, come Lord Jesus!" That's the attitude we should have about the Lord's return — one of hopeful expectancy any moment.

Some people are bothered by this promise. They ask, "How could Jesus have meant what He said? How could He really have meant He was returning 'soon'? After all, He spoke these words two thousand years ago!" Well, we must keep in mind that God sees time differently from us. He is not on a time-line like we are, with a past, a present, and a future. He is outside of time as we know it. The Bible says that, to Him, "a thousand years is like a day" (Ps. 90:4 and 2 Pet. 3:8). The way God sees time, Jesus made this promise only two days ago.

Hosea's Affirmation

You will find this concept in the Book of Hosea at the end of chapter 5. There, in verse 15, it says that a day will come when the Lord will depart this earth for what He calls, "My place," which, of course, is heaven. He then says that He will remain in heaven until the Jewish people "acknowledge their guilt and seek My face." We know from other scriptures that the Jews will not do that until the end of the Tribulation period (Zech. 12:10). And the Lord continues to make that very point. He says, "In their *affliction* they will earnestly seek Me." That's the Tribulation. Chapter 6 verse 1 records what the Jewish people will cry out at the end of the Tribulation. They will say, "Come, let us return to the Lord, for He has torn us [that's the Tribulation], but He will heal us; He has wounded us [that's the Tribulation again], but He will bandage us. He will revive us *after two days;* He will raise us up on the third day that we may live before Him" (emphasis added).

To summarize, these verses in Hosea say that a day will come when the Messiah will leave this earth and return to heaven. He will stay in heaven until the Jewish people in their affliction cry out to Him and accept Him as Messiah. Then, He will return. He will come at the end of "two days," and He will raise us up to live before Him for the third day — the Millennium. My friends we're at the end of that two-day period, we're at the end of that 2,000 years. *Jesus is coming soon. We're living on borrowed time!*

Other Signs

There are other indications that we are living in the period of the Lord's return. One of those is found in Matthew 24 where Jesus told the people to watch the fig tree, which is a symbol of Israel. He said when that fig tree blossoms again we will know that He's at the very gates of heaven, ready to return. For the past 450 years prophetic scholars have told people, "Watch Israel, watch Israel, watch Israel." People have responded with laughter, scorn, and ridicule. They have said, "Israel will never exist again." Well, nobody is laughing now because Israel was re-established on May 14, 1948. We know Jesus is at the very gates of heaven because He said in Matthew 24 that the generation that sees the re-establishment of Israel is the generation that will see all these things come to pass (Matt. 24:34). *We are the terminal generation.*

Another sign is found in Luke 21:24 where Jesus pronounced three prophecies. First, He said the Jews would "fall by the edge of the sword." That happened 40 years later in A.D. 70 when the Romans conquered Jerusalem under Titus. Second, Jesus prophesied in that same verse that the Jews would be "led captive into all the nations." That happened too when the last Jewish revolt was put down in A.D. 135. Now, pay particular attention to the third prophecy in the verse: "Jerusalem will be trampled under foot by the Gentiles until the times of the Gentiles are fulfilled." Jerusalem came under the Gentiles in A.D. 70 when it fell to the Romans. The Romans were followed by the Byzantines. Then came the Arabs, the Crusaders, the Mamlukes, the Turks, the British, and finally, the Jordanians.

But on June 7, 1967, praise God, the Jews reconquered the city of Jerusalem for the first time in 1,897 years. That's the sign Jesus told us to watch for.

The Urgency of the Hour

My friends, let me say it again: *We are living on borrowed time!* Jesus is coming soon! He said He would, and that promise of His means all, or it means nothing at all. If you have rejected Him, it means nothing to you; if you have accepted Him, it should mean everything.

Well, that's it. I hope you are convinced now that the Book of Revelation can be understood and is worthy of careful study.

All I have to say in conclusion is "Maranatha!" That's the prayer of the early church recorded in 1 Corinthians 16:22. It is an Aramaic expression that means, "Our Lord come!" Oh yes, come quickly Lord Jesus!

Chapter 3

Systematizing Revelation

F our men were engaged in a discussion of the Book of
Revelation. "I'm premillennial!" one announced with
confidence.

"I'm amillennial," countered the second.

"Well, I've recently become postmillennial," said the third.

The fourth fellow said nothing. After waiting a few mo-
ments, the other three turned to him and demanded to know
his prophetic system.

"Well," he said hesitantly, "I guess I would say that I'm
panmillennial."

"What does that mean?" the others inquired.

"It means," he responded, "that I haven't the foggiest idea
what the Book of Revelation means, but I do know one thing
for sure — God is in control. And therefore, I figure it will all
pan out in the end!"

A Prophetic Cop-out

This humorous story is really a sad commentary on the
Church. I say that because I have found that the story expresses a truth. You see, I have discovered that the majority
of Christians and their pastors are panmillennial.

Why is that sad? Because it is an admission of spiritual laziness. The person who says he is a panmillennialist is unwilling to spend the time to find out what God's Word says about the end times. God's Word is not panmillennial. It contains numerous prophecies in which God makes some glorious promises concerning the end times.

My colleague Dennis Pollock once said to me, "Those who claim to be panmillennial remind me of the Know-Nothing political party that existed in the United States before the Civil War. Its members took pride in knowing nothing about nothing!" That seems to be the mindset of panmillennialists, at least regarding Bible prophecy.

It is true that the apostle Paul wrote, "No eye has seen, nor ear heard, nor the heart of man conceived what God has prepared for those who love Him" (1 Cor. 2:9; RSV). But the very next verse says that God has revealed those things about the future through His Holy Spirit.

God's prophetic promises have been given to provide us with hope, and we desperately need hope in this pagan world. Discovering those promises and relating them to each other in some systematic way is hard work, but the payoff is like mining for jewels and discovering the mother lode.

The Necessity for Study

People often ask me, "Why didn't the Lord just make it crystal clear as to what will happen in the future? It would have saved us a lot of study and arguing."

Yes, it certainly seems that way. But we would have been left with a cold, lifeless manual, and considering the fallen nature of man, we would still have ended up arguing about the meaning of the words in that manual. In that regard, I am reminded of a lecture I heard several years ago about the meaning of the phrase "caught up" in 1 Thessalonians 4:17, where the passage says that when Jesus appears in the heavens, those living in Christ will be "caught up" to meet Him in the clouds. The scholar spent an hour analyzing the words and their context before finally concluding that the phrase meant what it said! But the reason he engaged in this seemingly meaningless academic exercise is because there are people who deny the plain sense meaning of that phrase.

Personally, I'm glad God avoided outlining the fundamental doctrines of the Bible in laundry list form. The way the truths are presented requires us to dig and study and meditate and pray — and then dig some more! It is a process that draws us into the Word and deeper into our relationship with the Lord. In the process, we grow spiritually.

Assembling the Parts

Because prophetic truths are scattered throughout the Bible and no one prophet has the overall picture, the truths must be pieced together like a jigsaw puzzle. This fact has always prompted students of prophecy to attempt to systematize the various prophecies to show how they relate to each other.

Again, the process is a difficult one. For example, in 2 Peter 3:10 we are told that when the Lord returns, "the earth and its works will be burned up." How do we reconcile that statement with Revelation 20 which says that the Lord's return will be followed by an earthly reign of 1,000 years? How can the Lord reign on an earth that has been "destroyed with intense heat"? (2 Pet. 3:10).

In like manner, Revelation 21:1 says God will supply "a new heaven and a new earth" at the end of the Lord's millennial reign. But Isaiah 65:17–25 seems to indicate that the new heaven and earth will be supplied before the Lord's reign begins. How are these passages to be reconciled? Can they be reconciled without spiritualizing their meaning?

Reconciling "Conflicts"

The answer to that question is always yes, because God's Word does not contradict itself. But reconciling passages that appear to conflict with each other requires careful study and thought.

Regarding the verses about the new earth when the Lord

returns, I wrestled for years with the enigmatic problem they present, believing there must be some way to reconcile them while accepting their plain sense meaning. The breakthrough came when I noticed a reference in 2 Peter 3:6 to the fact that the earth in Noah's time had been "destroyed by water." It suddenly occurred to me that this destruction did not bring an end to the earth. Rather, it changed its basic nature.

With that breakthrough, I began to search the Scriptures concerning what they say about the earth. One of my very first discoveries was the assertion that the earth is eternal (Ps. 78:69, 148:6, and Eccles. 1:4). This confirmed my finding that references to the earth's "destruction" are references to basic changes in its nature and do not refer to its ceasing to exist.

I finally concluded that there have been three earths in the past, and there will be two more in the future (see figure 1).

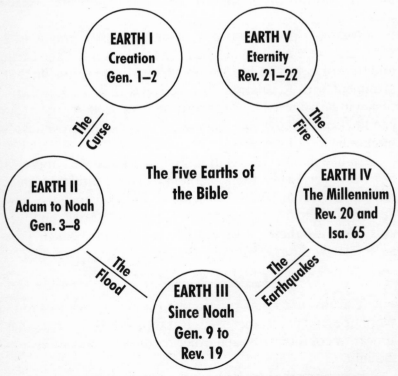

Figure 1: The Earth: Past, Present, and Future

The first earth was the perfect one created by God at the beginning of time. That earth was radically changed by the curse that God placed upon it when Adam and Eve sinned. The earth was radically changed again as a result of the Noahic flood.

Looking to the future, the earth will be changed again when Jesus returns. Revelation says a great earthquake will occur, so great that every valley will be lifted, every mountain will be lowered, and every island will be moved (Rev. 6:12–17 and 16:18–20). The whole topography of the earth will be changed, preparing the "new earth" for the Lord's reign, as prophesied in Isaiah 65:17–25.

The fifth and final earth will be provided at the end of the Millennium. God will consume the earth with fire to burn away the pollution of Satan's last revolt (2 Pet. 3:10). He will use that fire to reshape the earth like a hot ball of wax, and out of that inferno will come a new earth that will be returned to its original perfection (2 Pet. 3:13).

The Prophetic Perspective

Another significant part of the problem in reconciling Bible prophecy relates to what I would call "the prophetic perspective." When a prophet looks into the future, he's like a man looking down a mountain range. The man sees one mountaintop after another, representing major prophetic events. But he does not see the valleys separating the peaks. The valleys represent the time periods between the mountaintop events.

Figure 2: The Prophetic Perspective

The result of this unique perspective is that the prophet may speak of future events as if they occur in rapid succession, when in reality there are lengthy time periods between the events. Thus, in 2 Peter 3 the apostle sees the return of Jesus and then the destruction of the earth by fire. He is not given a vision of the intervening millennial reign of the Lord because it is not relevant to the point the Holy Spirit is trying to make in the passage. That point is that just as the earth was destroyed by water in the past, it will be destroyed by fire in the future, after the Lord returns. We learn from other passages that the fire will be 1,000 years after the Lord returns.

Prophetic Gaps

As you can see, this unique prophetic perspective produces prophetic gaps. A classic example of this telescopic or compressed vision of the prophets is to be found in Zechariah 9:9–10. In rapid succession the prophet describes three "mountain tops."

> **9** Rejoice greatly, O daughter of Zion!
> Shout in triumph, O daughter of Jerusalem!
> Behold, your king is coming to you;
> He is just and endowed with salvation,
> Humble, and mounted on a donkey,
> Even on a colt, the foal of a donkey.
>
> **10** I will cut off the chariot from Ephraim
> And the horse from Jerusalem;
> And the bow of war will be cut off.
> And He will speak peace to the nations;
> And His dominion will be from sea to sea,
> And from the River to the ends of the earth.

Notice that he begins in verse 9 with the Messiah's triumphal entry into Jerusalem, riding on a donkey. Then, at the beginning of verse 10, he refers to an event that took place

40 years later in A.D. 70 — namely, the temporary setting aside of Israel as a nation when Jerusalem was destroyed and the Jews were scattered worldwide. The latter part of verse 10 jumps to the indefinite future (it has now been almost 2,000 years) when the Lord will return to reign over all the world. In the passage, the events seem to occur immediately after each other. In reality, there are significant time gaps between them.

Jesus himself recognized that there are time gaps in prophetic passages. When He began His ministry at the synagogue in Nazareth, He read a prophecy about the Messiah from Isaiah 61 and then boldly proclaimed that He was the fulfillment (Luke 4:16–21). If you check the passage He read — Isaiah 61:1–2a — you will find that He stopped reading in the middle of a sentence because the rest of the sentence pertains to His second coming. The passage He quoted ends by saying the Messiah will "proclaim the favorable year of our God." Jesus read that part because He had come in love to die for the sins of mankind. The next phrase says that the Messiah will also come to proclaim "the day of vengeance of our God." Jesus did not read that phrase because it relates to His second coming.

Daniel's Gap

One of the most famous prophetic gaps in the Bible is the one located in Daniel's prophecy of the 70 weeks of years (Dan. 9:24–27). How do we know it contains a gap? Because the first verse in the prophecy says that God is going to accomplish six things among the Jewish people during a period of 490 years (Dan. 9:24). The first 69 weeks of years (483 years) will lead up to the coming of the Messiah and His "cutting off" — that is, His death. The final week of years (7 years) will start when "the prince who is to come" (a reference to the Antichrist) makes a covenant with Israel that will bring them peace and enable them to rebuild their temple.

There must be a gap between the first 483 years and the last 7 years because only one of the six things God said He would accomplish among the Jewish people during these weeks of years has been brought to completion — and that is "an atonement for iniquity." The other five goals are yet to be accomplished: ending the Jew's rejection of the Messiah, putting an end to their sins, bringing in everlasting righteousness, fulfilling all prophecy, and anointing a holy place (a new temple). All these goals will be accomplished during the 7 years of the Tribulation when the Jews will be brought to the end of themselves, causing them to repent and accept the Messiah, crying out, "Baruch haba bashem Adonai!" ("Blessed is He who comes in the name of the Lord!" — Matt. 23:39). At that point the world will be flooded with righteousness as the Lord begins His reign, and the millennial temple will be built.

Prefillment in Type

Another peculiarity of prophecy that produces differences in interpretation is the fact that it is often prefilled in symbolic type before it is completely fulfilled in history.

A classic example of this phenomenon is the well-known prophecy in Isaiah 7:14 about the Messiah's birth: "Behold, a virgin will be with child and bear a son, and she will call His name Immanuel" (Isa. 7:14). We often think of this prophecy as one that relates only to the future Messiah. But the context of the prophecy makes it clear that there was a prefillment in symbolic type at the time Isaiah lived.

You see, the city of Jerusalem was under siege by enemy forces. King Ahaz of Judah was deeply troubled, fearing the city would fall. God decided to give the king a sign that his capital city would not fall. The sign, which the prophet Isaiah gave to the king, was that a virgin would bear a son who would be named "Immanuel," meaning "God is with us." The implication of the passage is that such a child was born to a young woman who was a virgin at the time the prophecy was spoken. Many scholars believe the woman was most likely Isaiah's second wife (Isa. 8:1–4), the assumption being that his first wife died after the birth of their son Shear-jashub (Isa. 7:3). The birth of this child named Immanuel assured the king that God was with him and his people, and the city would not fall.

The Hebrew word used in the passage (*almah*) could be translated either "virgin" or "maiden" or "young woman," but 500 years later, about 250 years before the birth of Jesus, the Jewish sages who translated the Hebrew Scriptures into Greek, producing the Septuagint version, recognized this verse to be messianic in nature, and so they used a Greek word, *parthenos*, that could only be translated "virgin." They felt that the passage was a promise that the Messiah would be God in the flesh, and therefore the child would have to be born to a virgin.

Their perception was confirmed when the Holy Spirit prompted Matthew, in his gospel, to quote Isaiah's verse and apply it to the birth of Jesus (Matt. 1:23). In doing so, Matthew used the same Greek work that had been used in the Septuagint, a word that can only be translated "virgin."

Daniel's Prophecy Again

Another good example of the prefillment in type relates to Daniel's famous prophecy of the 70 weeks of years. In that prophecy Daniel states that a "prince who is to come" will stop the sacrifices in the temple and will set up an "abomination" that "makes desolate" (Dan. 9:27).

Almost 400 years later, in 168 B.C., a Syrian despot by the name of Antiochus Epiphanes entered Jerusalem, desecrated the temple, and stopped the sacrifices.[1] He also erected a statue of Zeus in the Holy Place of the temple.[2] He was a madman who was determined to stamp out Judaism. He seemed to be the fulfillment of Daniel's prophecy.

But 200 years later in about A.D. 31, Jesus referred to Daniel's prophecy in His Olivet Discourse and stated that its fulfillment was yet future (Matt. 24:15). I feel certain that Jesus' statement must have caught many in His audience by surprise. With this statement Jesus made it clear that Antiochus was a prefillment of Daniel's prophecy in symbolic type, not a fulfillment of it.

Matthew 24: History or Prophecy?

Preterists and some historicists argue that Daniel's prophecy and all the prophecies of Matthew 24 were fulfilled 40 years after Jesus's Olivet Discourse in A.D. 70 when the Romans destroyed Jerusalem. But I would maintain that what happened in A.D. 70 was just another prefillment of these prophecies in type.

Let's consider the evidence. Jesus said Daniel's prophecy would be fulfilled when "the abomination of desolation" is seen "standing in the holy place" (Matt. 24:15). This could be a reference to the Antichrist himself, but it is more likely a reference to some ungodly idol that will be erected. Unlike the tyrant Antiochus Epiphanes who desecrated the temple with a statue of Zeus, the Roman conqueror, Titus, took no such action in A.D. 70 before his troops destroyed the city and the temple.[3]

Jesus also stated that the fulfillment of the prophecy would be marked by a "great tribulation" for the Jewish people that would be the most intense in all of history, "since the beginning of the world until now, nor ever shall [be]" (Matt. 24:21). Those words were not fulfilled in A.D. 70. The slaughter of the Jews by Titus was severe, but it pales in comparison to what the Jews suffered during the Nazi Holocaust of World War II.

Furthermore, the prophet Zechariah tells us that during the end times a total of two-thirds of the Jewish people will die during a period of unparalleled calamity (Zech. 13:8–9). In other words, there is a period of Jewish persecution yet to occur that will even exceed the horrors of the Nazi Holocaust.

The third and decisive clue that Matthew 24 is yet to be fulfilled is found in verse 29 which says the Lord will return "immediately after the tribulation of those days." This statement clearly makes Matthew 24 a prophecy that is yet to be fulfilled. It is this statement that forces extreme, but consistent, preterists to argue that the second coming of Jesus actually occurred in A.D. 70! This fanciful assertion always reminds me of two fellows whom Paul condemned —

Hymenaeus and Philetus. They were confusing the saints by arguing that the resurrection of believers had already taken place (2 Tim. 2:17–18).

Reason for Disagreement

We have discovered many reasons for people to disagree when they start trying to systematize Bible prophecy. Prophecies can be wrenched out of context. Prophecies that seem to conflict can be ignored. Prophetic gaps in time can go unrecognized, and symbolic prefillments can be accepted as fulfillments.

Complicating matters further are the various viewpoints which people bring to the prophetic Scriptures concerning their nature and purpose. Is prophecy intended to give us a road map of future events as the futurists maintain? Or, is its purpose to give us a better understanding of contemporary events as the historicists contend? Does it relate only to Christians of the first century, as many preterists claim? Or, is it simply meant to be inspirational literature with no specific meaning, as the idealists contend?

Adding still more fuel to the fire of controversy is the basic argument about whether or not prophecy is to be interpreted literally or figuratively.

Even those who hold a similar viewpoint may disagree about the timing and placement of specific events. For example, among premillennialists (those who believe the Lord will come before the Millennium begins), there are some who put the Russian invasion of Israel (Ezek. 38 and 39) in the middle of the Tribulation, while there are others who place this invasion at the beginning of the Tribulation or shortly before the Tribulation begins.

Premillennialists have not even been able to agree on the timing of the Rapture. Some place it at the beginning of the Tribulation, others in the middle or near the end, and some even combine it with the Second Coming as all one event that will take place at the end of the Tribulation.

When all these various interpretive factors are taken into

account, it is no wonder that people have developed different systems for understanding end-time events. There are three basic systems that have been refined over the centuries, with variations within each one. The systems are called premillennial, amillennial, and postmillennial. Let's consider them in the order in which they developed historically.

Historic Premillennialism

The oldest viewpoint is called historic premillennialism. It is termed "historic" for two reasons: to differentiate it from modern premillennialism and to indicate that it was the historic position of the Early Church.

It is called "premillennial" because it envisions a return of Jesus to earth before (pre) the beginning of the Millennium. The word, millennium, is a combination of two Latin words — *mille* and *annum* — which, when put together, simply mean one thousand years.

A diagram of this viewpoint is presented in figure 3. The system divides the future of the world into four periods: 1) the current Church Age; 2) a seven-year period called the Tribulation; 3) a reign of Christ on earth lasting one thousand years (the Millennium); and 4) the eternal state when the Redeemed will dwell forever with God on a new earth.

This view is based on a literal interpretation of what the Bible says will happen in the end times. One of its distinctive features is that it places the Rapture of the Church at the end of the Tribulation, combining it with the Second Coming as one event.

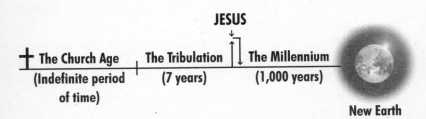

Figure 3: The Historic Premillennial System

According to this view, the Church will remain on earth during the Tribulation. At the end of that period, Jesus will appear in the heavens and the Church will be caught up to meet Him in the sky. The saints will be instantly glorified, and then they will immediately return to the earth to reign with Jesus for a thousand years.

The Church Fathers

This is the only systematic view of end-time events that existed during the first 300 years of the Church. With one notable exception, all the Church Fathers who expressed themselves on the topic of prophecy were premillennial until A.D. 400. Justin Martyr, who was born in A.D. 100, went so far in his writings on the subject as to suggest that anyone with a different viewpoint was heretical. Those today who disagree with this view respond to the near unanimity of the early Church Fathers by saying they were simply wrong in their interpretation of the prophetic Scriptures.

It certainly should be noted that these Early Church leaders were not prophetic scholars. They wrote very little on prophecy, and what they wrote was sketchy. Their main concern was not prophecy, but the deity of Jesus, the oneness of God, the practical problems of church organization, and survival amidst persecution.

Yet their concept of end-time events should not be dismissed out of hand as crude and primitive, for anyone who has studied the prophetic Scriptures will have to admit that the Church Fathers' viewpoint presents a plain sense summary of the Bible's teachings about the end times.

The major exception to the consensus opinion among the early Church Fathers was Origen (c. A.D. 185–254). Origen's approach to all of Scripture was to spiritualize it. He therefore denied the literal meaning of prophecy. He looked upon its language as highly symbolic and expressive of deep spiritual truths rather than of future historical events.[4]

Although Origen could not accept the premillennial viewpoint, he did not develop an alternative. That task fell to the most influential of the Church Fathers, St. Augustine (A.D. 358–434). He conceived an alternative system at the end of the fourth century.

Amillennialism

The concept formulated by Augustine is illustrated in figure 4. It is called amillennialism. This strange name derives from the fact that in the Greek language a word is negated by putting the letter "a" in front of it. Thus, amillennial literally means "no thousand years."

The term is misleading, however, because most amillennialists do believe in a millennium, but not a literal, earthly one. They argue that the Millennium is the current spiritual reign of Christ over the Church and that it will continue until He returns for His saints. They thus interpret the thousand years as a symbolic period of time.

One appealing aspect of the amillennial view is its simplicity. The Church Age comes to a screaming halt as a result of the Rapture of the Church. There is no Tribulation, no literal earthly Millennium, and no eternity on a new earth. Augustine spiritualized everything, arguing that the kingdom is the Church, the Millennium is the current Church Age, and the new earth is symbolic language for heaven. He further argued that the binding of Satan had taken place at the Cross, and the first resurrection is a spiritual one that occurs when a person puts his or her faith in Jesus.

By denying any future earthly kingdom of Christ, Augustine converted the Church into the millennial kingdom, with the implication that its leader is the vicar of Christ on

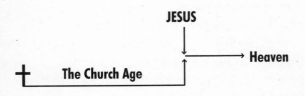

Figure 4: The Amillennial System

earth through whom the Lord rules. This concept greatly appealed to Church leaders and was quickly adopted as Church dogma at the Council of Ephesus in A.D. 431. It was later adopted by the Reformation leaders and has remained the majority viewpoint among mainline Protestant denominations. That means the Amillennial viewpoint is the one that is held today by the vast majority of all those who profess to be Christians, both Catholics and Protestants.

Postmillennialism

The third view of end time events, called postmillennialism, did not develop until the mid-17th century, long after the Reformation. The Reformation did not produce a new prophetic system because the Reformation leaders had their attention riveted on the questions of biblical authority and justification by faith. It is true that the Reformers applied the historicist approach to Revelation to make the book a tool for attacking the Catholic Church, but they continued to adhere to the amillennial system.

The postmillennial view was a product of the rationalistic revolution in thinking. It was developed in the mid-1600's by a Unitarian minister named Daniel Whitby (1638–1726).[5] It was immediately dubbed "postmillennialism" because it envisioned a return of Jesus after (post) a literal thousand year reign of the Church over all the earth. This view is illustrated in figure 5.

Postmillennialism spread quickly within the Protestant

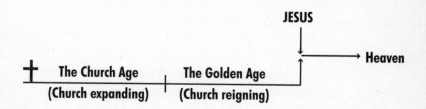

Figure 5: The Postmillennial System

world, probably for two reasons. First, it gave Protestants an opportunity to differ from the Catholic position. More importantly, it was a theological expression of the prevailing rationalistic philosophy of the age, a philosophy that boldly proclaimed the ability of mankind to build the kingdom of heaven on earth.

The postmillennial view holds that the Church Age will gradually evolve into a "golden age" when the Church will rule over all the world. This will be accomplished through the Christianization of the nations. At the end of that golden age, the Lord will appear, the Church will present the kingdom to Him, and earthly history will come to an end as the Church is taken to heaven to live eternally with the Lord.

To its credit, it can be said that this viewpoint served as a mighty stimulus to missionary efforts during the 18th and 19th centuries. Missionaries were seized with the vision of speeding up the return of the Lord by preaching the gospel to all the world.

A Sudden Death

By the end of the 19th century, nearly all segments of Protestant Christianity had adopted the postmillennial viewpoint. As the 20th century approached, there was high anticipation that it would prove to be "the Christian Century" when the Church would triumph over all the nations and the golden age would begin. Those hopes were to be quickly dashed, and the postmillennial view was to be quickly dropped.

Postmillennialism died almost overnight with the outbreak of the First World War. The reason, of course, is that this great war undermined one of the fundamental assumptions of the postmillennial viewpoint — the assumption of the inevitability of progress. This had always been a fatal flaw in the postmillennial concept, due mainly to its birth in rationalistic humanism. Its visions of the perfectibility of man and the redemption of society were destroyed by the atrocities of the war.

Another fatal flaw of the postmillennial system was its lack of a consistent biblical base. To expound the view, it was necessary to literalize some prophecies (those concerning the Millennium) while at the same time spiritualizing other prophecies (the personal presence of the Lord during the Millennium). Also, it was necessary to ignore or explain away the many prophecies in the Bible that clearly state that society is going to get worse rather than better as the time approaches for the Lord's return (Matt. 24:4–24 and 2 Tim. 3:1–5).

The postmillennial view also ignored the fact that the Bible teaches that the Church will never Christianize the world because the great majority of people will always reject the gospel. Jesus made this clear in His parable of the sower (Matt. 13:3–30) where He indicated that only one in four will truly respond to the gospel. He made it even clearer when He stated, "The gate is wide, and the way is broad that leads to destruction, and many are those who enter by it. For the gate is small, and the way is narrow that leads to life, and few are those who find it" (Matt. 7:13–14).

A Protestant Vacuum

The sudden death of postmillennialism left a prophetic vacuum among Protestant groups. Since the postmillennial view was based to a large extent upon a spiritualizing approach to Scripture, most Protestant groups returned to the spiritualized amillennial viewpoint they had abandoned in the 1700s.

A factor that encouraged this move of Protestants toward amillennialism was the increasing influence of the German School of Higher Criticism among mainline Protestant denominations. This school of thought hit the American Church like a bomb during the early years of the 20th century. It undermined the faith of many with its thesis that the Bible is not the inspired Word of God but is, instead, man's search for God, and is therefore full of myth, legend, and superstition. As this blasphemous concept gained influence, it led to people rejecting any literal interpretation of the Scriptures. Christian leaders began to spiritualize everything, including the virgin birth, the miracles of Jesus, His resurrection and, of course, His promise to return again.

However, a new choice of prophetic viewpoint presented itself on the American scene about this same time, and some of the more fundamentalist Protestant groups opted for it. They did so because it was based on a literal interpretation of Scripture. This view was technically called "dispensational premillennialism" because it originated with a group who had been nicknamed "Dispensationalists." I call it the modern premillennial viewpoint.

Modern Premillennialism

This method of systematizing end-time Bible prophecies crystallized in the early 1800s among a group in England known as the Plymouth Brethren. The view is illustrated in figure 6.

As can be readily seen, this viewpoint revives the historic premillennial view except for its concept of the Rapture of the Church. The Plymouth Brethren envisioned two future comings of Jesus, one *for* His church and one *with* His church. The Lord would appear in the heavens *for* His church before the beginning of the Tribulation. He would return to the earth *with* His church at the end of the Tribulation. The appearing was called the Rapture; the return to earth, the Second Coming. Their concept of the Rapture has since come to be known as the "pre-Tribulation Rapture."

This viewpoint has been attacked as being "too new to be true." But its advocates are quick to point out that the Bible teaches the principle of "progressive illumination" regarding

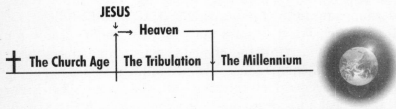

Figure 6: The Modern Premillennial System

prophecy (Dan. 12:4 and Jer. 30:24). What they mean by this is that the Bible itself indicates that end-time prophecy will be better understood as the time nears for its fulfillment. That's due, of course, to historic developments (like the re-establishment of Israel) and technological innovations (like computers and nuclear power).

My own personal attempt to systematize the Book of Revelation and other end-time prophecies is presented in figure 7, on page 120. It is based upon the modern premillennial concept, with the Rapture placed before the Tribulation begins. It assumes that the Tribulation events portrayed in Revelation are sequential in nature except for flash-forwards that are inserted to remind us that Jesus is going to triumph in the end. The flash-forwards are indicated on the chart by the arrows that point from the seal and trumpet judgments toward the end of the Tribulation.

Comparisons

Looking back over these various views of the end times, we can see some significant differences. But let's not overlook the similarities. All agree that Jesus is coming back for His saints. All agree that the Redeemed will spend eternity in the presence of God. These two points of agreement are far more important than the many points of disagreement.

Still, the areas of disagreement are significant. Two of the views (the amillennial and postmillennial) deny that Jesus will ever manifest His glory before the nations in a worldwide reign of peace, justice, and righteousness. The postmillennial view also denies the soon coming of the Lord, for according to this view, the Lord cannot return until His Church has ruled over the world for a thousand years.

The key to the differences is the approach to Scripture. If you tend to spiritualize Scripture, you will end up with an amillennial or postmillennial viewpoint. If you tend to accept Scripture for its plain sense meaning, you will have a premillennial viewpoint.

Figure 7: An Overview of Tribulation Events

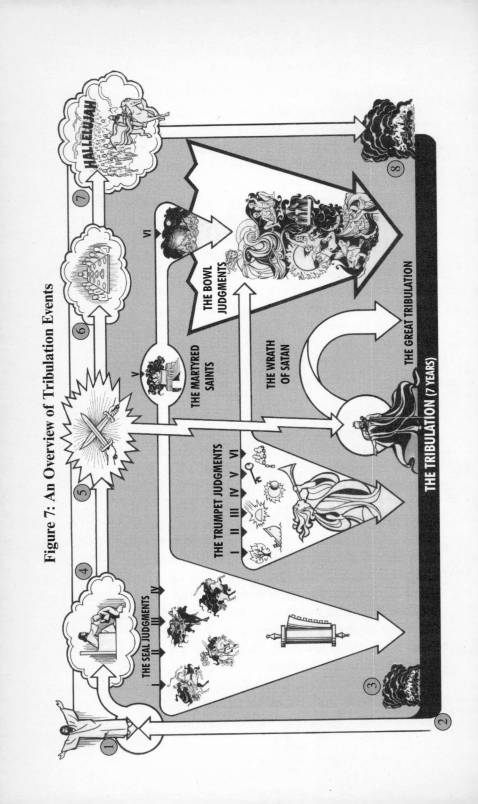

1. **The appearing of Jesus (John 14:1–3).**
2. **The rapture of the Saints.** The dead in Christ will rise first. The living in Christ will be translated (1 Thess. 4:13–18 and 1 Cor. 15:51–55).
3. **The Russian invasion of Israel.** Russia will be supernaturally destroyed on the hills of Israel (Ezek. 38 and 39).
4. **The judgment of believers.** The works of believers will be judged to determine degrees of reward (2 Cor. 5:10). The judgment of believers for their sins has already occurred at the cross (see 2 Cor. 5:21; John 5:24; Gal. 3:13; and Isa. 53:5–6).
5. **The war in heaven.** Satan will be cast to earth (Rev. 12:7–12).
6. **The marriage of Jesus and His bride (Rev. 19:7–9).**
7. **The return of Jesus in glory (Rev. 19:11–16).**
8. **The Battle of Armageddon (Joel 3:13–16 and Rev. 19:17–21).**

Figure 7: An Overview of Tribulation Events

Amillennial Problems

Because the amillennial system is the predominant one in Christendom today, I think it warrants closer examination.

The first thing that needs to be emphasized about this view is that its developer, St. Augustine, "platonized the prophetic Scriptures." By this, I mean he read and interpreted Bible prophecy as if it had been written by Greek philosophers rather than Hebrew prophets. Keep in mind that the Greeks had a creation-negating viewpoint. They viewed the material world as essentially evil. In contrast, the Hebrew view contained in the Scriptures is creation-affirming. To the Hebrew mind, the creation is basically good, even though it has been corrupted by man's sin and the Curse. Thus, the Psalmist writes, "The heavens are telling of the glory of God; and their expanse is declaring the work of His hands" (Ps. 19:1).

Whereas the Greeks looked toward the dissolution of the universe, the Hebrews yearned for the redemption of the creation. Isaiah dreamed of "the new heavens and the new earth" (Isa. 66:22), and Paul wrote that the whole creation is longing for its redemption so that it will "be set free from its slavery to corruption" (Rom. 8:18–21).

Augustine's Greek world view would not allow him to accept at face value what the Bible said about end-time events. What the Bible prophesied was too much tied to this world — a future kingdom of Christ on this earth and eternity with God on a new earth.

Using the spiritualizing approach, Augustine tried to explain away the Tribulation, the Millennium and the new earth. The result was the amillennial viewpoint of end-time events which holds that the current Church Age will end abruptly with the Rapture of the Church. At that point the redeemed will be resurrected in spiritual bodies, the unrighteous will be consigned to hell, the material universe will cease to exist, and the redeemed will take up residence with God in an ethereal heaven.

Augustine's radical new system provided some philosophical advantages to a Church that was struggling to assert itself. By adopting the amillennial concept, the Church could argue that it was the kingdom of God on earth that should rule over the nations. But the view raised some very serious theological questions because it so clearly violated what the Bible literally taught about the end times. Let's consider some of those questions.

Where Is the Millennium?

This is a rather obvious question, but Augustine's answer was surprising. Instead of denying outright that there would ever be a Millennium, he argued instead that the Millennium began at the Cross and would continue a thousand years until the return of Jesus. Later, when the Lord failed to return after a thousand years, amillennialists simply spiritualized the thousand years to mean an indefinite period of time from the Cross to the Second Coming.

Note carefully that Augustine did not deny the Millennium; he simply redefined it to mean the spiritual reign of Christ through the Church during the Church Age.

That means we are in the Millennium now and have been for almost 2,000 years, and that creates a major problem for amillennialists. For you see, when you read the Bible's prophecies about the Millennium, there is no correspondence between them and the reality of the world in which we live.

We live in a world that is rotten to the core. The Bible says that during the Millennium, "The earth will be flooded with the knowledge of the glory of the Lord as the waters cover the sea" (Isa. 11:9; Hab. 2:14). The nations of the world today are all in rebellion against God and His anointed One. The prophecies say that during the Millennium the nations will all be in subjection to the Lord and will glorify His name (Ps. 22:27–31). If the Lord is reigning over the nations of the world today, He is doing a very poor job of it. Isaiah says that when the Lord reigns, the world will be characterized by peace, righteousness, and justice (Isa. 9:7).

The amillennial response to this is usually to argue that we are in the Millennium because the Holy Spirit is in the world restraining evil. If the Holy Spirit were not here, things would be much worse. Thus, relatively speaking, we are in the Millennium. But the Bible doesn't speak in relative terms about the Millennium. It states absolutely that there will be international peace, justice, righteousness and lovingkindness (Hos. 2:18–20).

Where Is the Tribulation?

Augustine gave a startling response to this question. He said that we are simultaneously in both the Millennium and the Tribulation! We are in the Millennium because the Holy Spirit is restraining evil, but we are also in the Tribulation because the Church will suffer persecution until the Lord returns.

When it was pointed out that the Bible says the Tribulation will last only seven years, Augustine dismissed the number as symbolic. He argued that the number seven represents a complete period of time, and therefore it represents the period from the Cross to the Second Coming.

It is true that the Church will always suffer tribulation in this world, but the Bible teaches there is going to be a special time of unparalleled tribulation that will come upon the world in the end times (Deut. 4:30). We are told it will affect the whole world (Isa. 24) and the Jews in particular (Jer. 30:4–7).

With regard to the seven-year length of the Tribulation, this number of years is not specifically mentioned in Revelation. Instead, Revelation 11:3 says the ministry of the two witnesses in Jerusalem will last "1,260 days" (3-1/2 years according to a prophetic year of 360 days). Revelation 13:5 then states that following their murder, the Antichrist will rule for an additional "42 months" (another 3-1/2 years). This latter period of time is confirmed in Revelation 12:6 where we are told that God will protect a Jewish remnant from the Antichrist by nourishing them in the wilderness for 1,260 days (3-1/2 years). This is reiterated in Revelation 12:14 where the time period for the remnant's nourishment is stated to be "a time and times and half a time," which is a Jewish colloquialism for 3-1/2 years.

As you can see, these time periods are precisely defined and are carefully related to Tribulation events. To dismiss them as symbolic simply because they add up to seven is flippant, to say the least. Furthermore, the seven-year length of the Tribulation that is specified in Revelation is not new information. It is simply an affirmation of Daniel's prophecy that God would finish His work among the Jews during the 70th week of years — which is a period of seven years (Dan. 9:27).

The Book of Revelation says that the Tribulation will be a special, concentrated period of the pouring out of God's wrath. In fact, it says that during the first three and a half years, over one-half the population of the earth will die! The world has never experienced calamities of such magnitude.

Is Satan Bound?

This is a very critical question because the Bible says that Satan will be bound at the beginning of the Millennium (Rev. 20:1–3). Augustine argued that Satan was bound at the Cross. I was making this point at a conference one day when a member of the audience suddenly jumped to his feet and said,

"Brother, let me tell you something. If Satan was bound at the Cross, then he was bound with a very long chain, because he is always gnawing on my leg!"

Let's keep in mind that there is a sense in which Satan has always been bound. He is not omnipotent. He is not free to do anything he desires. The Book of Job reveals that Satan could not touch Job without God's permission.

It is true that Satan was further bound by the Cross. The reason is that since that time believers in Jesus have received the indwelling power of the Holy Spirit, enabling them to be overcomers in their combat with Satan. The Word says, "He who is within us is greater than he who is in the world" (1 John 4:4).

But the limitations which the Cross placed on Satan do not constitute the binding of Satan that the Scriptures say will take place at the beginning of the Millennium. Revelation says Satan will be bound in a special way so that he can no longer "deceive the nations" (Rev. 20:3). How can anyone argue that the nations are not deceived today? They are definitely deceived, and thus Satan is not bound. He is still the "ruler of this world" (John 16:11).

Where Are the Two Resurrections?

The Bible says there will be two resurrections, one of the just and another of the unjust (Acts 24:15). It further states that these two resurrections will be separated by a thousand years (Rev. 20:5–6). The amillennial view has only one resurrection, occurring at the end of the Church Age.

Augustine "solved" this problem by spiritualizing the first resurrection. He said the first resurrection is a spiritual one that occurs when a person accepts Jesus as Lord and is born again. The second resurrection is the one that will occur when the Lord returns and everyone, both the just and the unjust, will be resurrected from the dead.

This exercise in imaginative interpretation shows what happens when you start spiritualizing. Scripture starts meaning whatever you want it to mean. In this case, the first resurrection is declared to be a spiritual one, but the second resurrection is interpreted to be a literal, physical one. Who says? Man does, not the Bible.

Where Is the New Earth?

Augustine also spiritualized this concept. He argued that the "new earth" mentioned in Revelation 21 was simply a symbol for heaven.

But as I have already pointed out earlier in this chapter, the Bible teaches that the earth is eternal. Psalm 148:6 says that the creation has been established forever and that the Lord has decreed it will never pass away. Psalm 78:69 says the Lord has founded the earth forever. In Luke 21:33 Jesus said, "Heaven and earth will pass away," but He meant that in the sense that Peter tells us that the heavens and earth will be consumed with fire in order to be replaced by "new heavens and a new earth" (2 Pet. 3:10–13).

The Bible never speaks of the material universe coming to an end. Rather, it promises over and over that this earth, including the plant and animal kingdoms, will be redeemed. It is all going to be restored to its original perfection. Read Isaiah 11:6–9 and Romans 8:18–23.

Revelation 21 tells us point blank that the redeemed are going to live eternally in a New Jerusalem located on a new earth. Further, it says that God is going to come down to the new earth and live with us. The Bible never speaks of us living eternally with God in heaven. To spiritualize all this is to make a mockery of Scripture.

Is God Finished with the Jews?

Amillennialists claim that "God washed His hands of the Jews" because of their unbelief, and He therefore has no purpose left for them. This is a pernicious doctrine that has led to much anti-Semitism. The fact of the matter is that the Jews are still the Chosen People of God, and the Lord intends to fulfill every promise He has ever made to them as a nation.

The Book of Romans makes all this very clear. In Romans 3:1–4 Paul asks a rhetorical question: "Has the unfaithfulness of the Jews nullified God's faithfulness to them?" For almost its entire history, the Church has said "Yes!" What does Paul say? His answer is, "May it never be!"

Likewise, in Romans 11:1 Paul asks, "Has God rejected His people?" Again, for almost two thousand years the Church has answered, "Yes!" But what does Paul say in response to his question? He says, "May it never be!" And then he adds, "God has not rejected His people whom He foreknew" (Rom. 11: 2). He then proceeds to explain that a great remnant of the Jews will be saved in the end times (Rom. 9:27; 11:25–32).

The Jewish people have been set aside as a result of God's discipline. But He has not forgotten them. In Isaiah 49:16 the Lord says He could never forget the Jewish people because He has them tattooed on the palms of His hands! In Jeremiah 31:35–37 the Lord asks, "When will the offspring of Israel cease to be a nation before Me?" His answer is that they will continue to be special in His eyes until the fixed order of the universe departs or until the day all the heavens and all the oceans have been fully explored. In Romans 11:29 Paul says that the "gifts and calling of God are irrevocable." And in Romans 9:1–5 he speaks of promises to the Jews that God fully intends to fulfill.

That's the reason the Jews are being regathered from the four corners of the world right now. It is one of the greatest miracles of history. The Lord intends to provoke them to repentance by bringing all the nations of the world against them (Zech. 12:1–3). When they become totally desperate, they will look to the Lord for their salvation. That is when they will repent. They will "look on Him whom they have pierced, and they will mourn" (Zech. 12: 10). And on that glorious day, a fountain of salvation will be opened for the house of David (Zech. 13:1).

God will then establish these believing Jews as the prime nation of the world during the Millennium, and through them He will once again bless all the nations on earth (Isa. 60–62).

Has the Church Fulfilled the Kingdom Promises?

There is no doubt that the Church is God's kingdom on the earth today. But the Bible does not teach that the concept of the kingdom of God is limited solely to the Church.

I believe a review of Scripture shows that God has always had a kingdom upon this earth, but it has been manifested in different ways. The kingdom was originally expressed in the creation itself (Ps. 93:1–2), through its perfect obedience to God's will. When the creation was corrupted through the sin of man, the kingdom became expressed in the lives of the patriarchs who, like Job, responded obediently in faith to God's will. The kingdom became focused in a more tangible manner after the call of Abraham and the emergence of the nation of Israel (Exod. 19:6).

Since Pentecost, the kingdom has been expressed in the institution of the Church (Col. 1:13). But the Bible promises different expressions of the kingdom in the future — first, in the form of a thousand year rule of Jesus upon this earth (Rev. 2:26–27), and second, in the form of an eternal rule of God upon a new earth (1 Cor. 15:24–28).

The kingdom is past, present, and future. It is currently expressed in the Church, but it is like a rose in the bud, yet to bloom in its full glory. The kingdom has always been coming, and it will continue to come until God's will is done perfectly on earth as it is in heaven. Even during the millennial reign of Jesus, the kingdom will be coming, for the Bible teaches that rebellion will be lurking in the hearts of men (Rev. 20:7–10). The consummation of the kingdom will not come until all enemies of God have been subdued. That will occur at the end of the millennial reign of Jesus, at which time He will surrender the kingdom to His Father, and God himself will reign forever over a redeemed creation (1 Cor. 15:24–28).

A Summary of Amillennial Problems

The amillennial view is based on a spiritualizing approach to Scripture which contends that the Bible does not mean what it says. It is a consistent view for theological liberals who also spiritualize the creation week, the miracles, the virgin birth, and the resurrection of Jesus. But what is astounding is the number of conservative Christians who endorse this view. In effect, they take the position that the Bible always means what it says unless it is talking about the second coming of Jesus!

The amillennial view does not stand the test of either the Scriptures or reality:

- How can anyone truly believe that we are currently living in the Millennium? Society is disintegrating before our eyes, and the Bible says it will get worse the closer we come to the Lord's return (2 Tim. 3:1–5).

- How can anyone truly believe that Satan is bound today? The Bible says, "The whole world lies in the power of the evil one" (1 John 5:19).

- How can anyone truly believe that the Church is reigning with Christ over the nations? Try telling that to persecuted and suffering Christians all over the world.

- How could anyone truly believe God has no purpose left for the Jews? After 2,000 years of dispersion all over the world, they are being regathered to Israel in what Jeremiah calls a miracle greater than the deliverance from Egyptian captivity (Jer. 16:14–15).

Let's stop playing games with God's Word. Let's allow it to mean what it says. I urge you to accept the plain sense meaning of Scripture. Don't play games with God's Word by spiritualizing it. When you do so, you can make it mean whatever you want it to mean, but in the process you will lose the true meaning that God intended.

Remember, the First Coming prophecies meant what they said. That should be our guide for interpreting the prophecies of the Second Coming.

Amillennial Conclusions

Does it really make any difference what you believe about the end times? Certainly it matters what you believe about Bible prophecy. It matters what you believe about anything, because your beliefs determine the way you live.

I grew up in an amillennial church, and the result was that I lived with little hope because I did not know about God's glorious promises concerning the future. I never looked forward to the Lord's return because I had no idea what was going to happen when He burst from the skies. I had no eternal perspective, and I had no appreciation of the continuing significance of the Jewish people.

When I began to study and believe Bible prophecy, my hope surged, and I was motivated as never before to live a holy life and to share the gospel with as many people as possible, as quickly as possible. I began yearning for the Lord's return because I became dissatisfied with this world. And I developed an even greater appreciation of God's unfathomable grace as I marveled over His continuing love for Israel.

What you believe about Bible prophecy has no effect on where you are going to spend eternity; it is not related to your justification. But it has an immediate impact upon your sanctification, upon how you walk before the Lord in this life. As the apostle John put it: "Everyone who has his hope fixed on Him purifies himself, just as He is pure" (1 John 3:3).

A Bothersome Question

When my study of Bible prophecy started leading me away from the amillennial viewpoint that I had grown up with, one question continued coming to my mind. I kept asking myself, "Why would God want His Son to return to this sin-sick world to reign for a thousand years? What purpose would the Millennium serve?" It really bothered me. The Word seemed to clearly teach that the Lord is coming back to this earth to reign for a thousand years. But I kept asking, "Why?"

I have since discovered that most amillennialists feel that same way. "Why," they will ask, "would the Lord want to come back to this rotten world? What could possibly be His purpose in returning to this world to reign for a thousand years? Why does God or the world need a Millennium?"

My study of the Word has led me to conclude that God has several vitally important purposes for the Millennium.

Promises to the Jews

The first reason there must be a Millennium is that God has made promises to the Jews which He will fulfill during that time.

God has promised that He will gather to the land of Israel the remnant of Jews who accept Jesus as their Messiah at the end of the Tribulation (Ezek. 36:22–28 and Zech. 10:6–9). He will pour out His Spirit upon this remnant (Isa. 32:15; 44:3), greatly expand their numbers and their land (Ezek. 36:10–11; 48:1–29), and make them the prime nation in all the world (Isa. 60–62). They will serve as an object lesson of the grace and mercy which God bestows upon those who turn to Him in repentance: "And it will come about that just as you were a curse among the nations, O house of Judah and house of Israel, so I will save you that you may become a blessing" (Zech. 8:13).

Zechariah says the blessings of God upon the Jewish remnant will be so great in those days that "ten men from all the nations will grasp the garment of a Jew saying, 'Let us go with you, for we have heard that God is with you' " (Zech. 8:23).

Promises to the Church

A second reason for the Millennium relates to a promise which God has made to the Church. God has promised that the Redeemed in Christ will reign over all the nations of the world. This promise was given through the prophet Daniel in the following words:

> Then the sovereignty, the dominion, and the greatness of all the kingdoms under the whole heaven will be given to the people of the saints of the Highest One; His kingdom will be an everlasting kingdom, and all the dominions will serve and obey Him (Dan. 7:27).

In the New Testament, Paul repeated the same promise in the simplest of terms: "If we endure, we shall also reign with Him" (2 Tim. 2:12). Jesus affirmed the promise in His letter to the church at Thyatira when He wrote, "And he who overcomes, and he who keeps My deeds until the end, to him I will give authority over the nations; and he shall rule them with a rod of iron" (Rev. 2:26–27).

When John was taken to heaven for a visit to the throne room of God, he heard the heavenly host singing a song that contained the following verse: "And You have made them [the redeemed] to be a kingdom and priests to our God; and they will reign upon the earth" (Rev. 5:10). This promise to the Church of worldwide dominion is going to be fulfilled during the Millennium. That is what Jesus was referring to in the Sermon on the Mount when He said, "Blessed are the gentle, for they shall inherit the earth" (Matt. 5:5).

Jesus will reign as king of the world from Mt. Zion in Jerusalem (Isa. 24:23 and Zech. 14:9). The redeemed, in their glorified bodies, will help Him with His reign by serving worldwide as administrators, judges, and spiritual tutors to those who enter the kingdom in the flesh — and to their children (Dan. 7:18, 27; Jer. 3:15; Luke 19:11–17).

Promises to the Nations

God has promised that a time will come when the nations will be provided with their greatest dream — namely, worldwide peace. This has been an international dream since the beginning of time, but it has proved to be impossibly elusive.

Peace conference after peace conference has been held. Multiple treaties have been signed. World organizations have been formed. Yet, war continues to ravage the nations.

God has promised to give mankind and the earth a rest from its wars. But that peace will not come until the Prince of Peace returns. Only then will the nations "hammer their swords into plowshares, and their spears into pruning hooks." Only then will we realize the dream of a world where "nation will not lift up sword against nation, and never again will they learn war" (Isa. 2:4).

God has promised that He will flood the earth with peace, righteousness, justice, and holiness: "The earth will be full of the knowledge of the Lord as the waters cover the sea" (Isa. 11:9).

Even the bells on horses' bridles and the pots in the kitchens will bear the inscription "Holy to the Lord" (Zech. 14:20–21).

These glorious promises of peace and rest and righteousness will be fulfilled during the Millennium.

Promises to the Creation

God has also made promises to His creation which He will fulfill during the Millennium.

God has promised to remove the curse which He placed upon the creation due to the sin of man. He has promised to deliver the creation from its bondage to decay and to restore it to its original beauty, balance, and peace (Rom. 8:18–23).

The carnivorous animals will become herbivorous (Isa. 11:6). The deadly animals will cease to be poisonous (Isa. 11:8–9). The plant kingdom will flourish and produce bountifully (Isa. 35 and Ezek. 34:25–31). The land of Israel will be so radically transformed that visitors will proclaim in amazement, "This desolate land has become like the garden of Eden" (Ezek. 36:35).

This is the reason Peter referred to the Lord's return as "the period of restoration of all things" (Acts 3:21). And it is the reason that in Old Testament times, when the high priest would go into the Holy of Holies once a year to sprinkle blood on the mercy seat of the ark of the covenant, he would also sprinkle blood on the ground in front of the ark (Lev. 16:15). The blood on the mercy seat was a symbolic prophecy that the blood of the Messiah would one day make it possible for the law of God (on tablets inside the ark) to be covered by the mercy of God. The blood on the ground pointed to the fact that the Messiah's sacrifice was for the redemption of all creation, and not just for man.

Promises to Jesus

The most important reason for the Millennium is that God is going to use it to fulfill promises which He has made to His Son. God has promised Jesus that He will be glorified in history to compensate in part for His humiliation in history. The Bible says point blank that Jesus will return to manifest His glory (Isa. 24:23; 66:18–19; 2 Thess. 1:7–10).

God also has promised that He will give Jesus dominion over all the world and that He will reign over the nations from Mt. Zion in Jerusalem (Dan. 7:13–14; Isa. 2:2–4; Zech. 14:1–9).

Psalm 2 presents a good summary of these promises. It begins by surveying the rebellion of the world's political leaders against God and His Son, referred to in the passage as "His Anointed" (verses 1–2). It describes their contempt for the Lord (verse 3).

But the psalm says that God sits in the heavens and laughs and scoffs at them because He has appointed a day of reckoning when He will "terrify them in His fury" (verse 5). That will be the day when He installs Jesus as "King upon Zion" (verse 6).

Jesus then speaks and tells of the promise that His Father has made to Him:

> I will surely tell of the decree of the Lord: He said to Me, "You are My Son, Today I have begotten You. Ask of Me, and I will surely give the nations as Your inheritance, and the very ends of the earth as Your possession. You shall break them with a rod of iron . . ." (Ps. 2:7–9).

It must be kept in mind that Jesus is currently a "king-in-waiting." Like King David, who had to wait many years after he was anointed before he became king of Israel, Jesus has been anointed King of kings and Lord and lords, but He has not yet begun to rule. He is currently serving as our high priest before the throne of God (Heb. 8:1). He is waiting for His Father's command to return and claim all the kingdoms of this world (Heb. 2:5–9 and Rev. 19:11–16).

A Final Reason

There is one other purpose for the Millennium that should be noted. I believe God is going to use the Millennium to prove to man once and for all that Satan's religion of humanism is totally bankrupt.

All humanists, regardless of their political or theological

labels, are agreed that the source of evil in the world is external to man. They view evil as rooted in the corruption of society. They believe that the solution to all man's problems can be found in societal reform.

Take, as an example, their attitude toward crime. They believe society is the root cause of crime. All we have to do to eliminate crime, they argue, is to provide people with a guaranteed job that will supply them with sufficient income so that they will be able to live in a nice suburb.

But such reforms do not transform the basic nature of people. In the ghetto a man will pay $25 for a prostitute. In the suburb he will chase his neighbor's wife. In the ghetto he will throw a rock through a window and steal a TV set. In the suburb he will put on his three-piece suit, drive to the office, manipulate the computer and embezzle a million dollars.

You do not change people's basic nature by changing their environment. Changing their environment simply converts them into more sophisticated sinners.

The humanist view is absolutely contrary to Scripture. The Word of God teaches that the source of evil is rooted within man's fallen nature, and that it is man, and not society, which needs to be changed (Gen. 8:21; Jer. 17:9–10; Mark 7:20–23). The Word also teaches that the only way this change can take place is through the work of the Holy Spirit within a person who has put his faith in Jesus.

God is going to prove this point by using the Millennium like a great experimental laboratory. He is going to place mankind in a perfect environment of peace and prosperity for a thousand years. Satan will be bound. Righteousness will abound.

Yet, at the end, when Satan is released, most people will rally to him when he calls the nations to rebellion against Jesus (Rev. 20:7–10). The Millennium will prove that what man needs is not a new society but a new heart.

Essential to the Master Plan

The Millennium is essential for the fulfillment of all the promises that God has made to the Jews, the Church, the nations, and the creation.

It is also essential to His determination to prove that the source of all evil is the fallen nature of man, not the corruption of society, and that the only hope for this world is Jesus, not political reform. Most important, the Millennium is essential to God's purpose in glorifying His Son. He is going to manifest the glory of Jesus before His redeemed saints and before all the nations of the world.

> All the ends of the earth will remember and turn to the Lord, and all the families of the nations will worship before You. For the kingdom is the Lord's, and He rules over the nations. . . . Posterity will serve Him; it will be told of the Lord to the coming generation. They will come and will declare His righteousness to a people who will be born, that He has performed it (Ps. 22:27–31).

God's Faithfulness

The Creator of this universe is a covenant making God who is faithful to all His promises. He cannot lie (Heb. 6:18). He cannot forget a promise (Deut. 4:31). He is faithful even when we are unfaithful (2 Tim. 2:13).

When the angel Gabriel appeared to Mary to announce to her that she would be the mother of the Messiah, he said:

> Behold, you will conceive in your womb and bear a son, and you shall call His name Jesus. He will be great, and will be called the Son of the Most High; and the Lord God will give to Him the throne of His father, David; and He will reign over the house of Jacob forever; and of His kingdom there will be no end (Luke 1:31–33).

This magnificent statement contains seven promises. Four of them relate to the first advent of the Lord, and they have all been fulfilled. Mary did conceive and bear a son. His name was called Jesus. He was great, and He was called the Son of God.

The last three promises which Gabriel made to Mary have not been fulfilled. They relate to the second coming of Jesus:

1) He will be given the throne of David.
2) He will reign over the house of Jacob.
3) There will be no end to His kingdom.

I call these three promises "The Forgotten Promises of Christmas" because they are overlooked when the Christmas story is taught today in most churches.

Spiritualizing

Amillennialists argue that these promises have been fulfilled. But to sustain that argument, they must spiritualize their meaning. Thus, they contend that Jesus is now on the throne of David; that the "house of Jacob" is the Church; and that Jesus' current reign over the Church is eternal.

There is no doubt that Jesus is currently reigning from His father's throne over His kingdom, the Church. But to identify that reign with the one promised to Mary takes a great leap of imagination.

The "throne of David" is not the throne of God. The throne of God is in heaven. The throne of David is in Jerusalem (Ps. 122:5). Jesus himself clearly differentiates between the throne of God and His own throne in Revelation 3:21. In that verse, Jesus says that He will one day allow believers to sit with Him on His throne just as His Father has allowed Him to share His throne.

Jesus is not on the throne of David today. He is sitting at the right hand of His Father, on His Father's throne. He will occupy the throne of David when He returns to earth to reign over all the nations of the world from Mount Zion in Jerusalem (Isa. 24:21–23).

The "house of Jacob" is not the Church. This is an Old Testament term for the Children of Israel (Exod. 19:3). The Church is never referred to in Scripture as the house of Jacob. The Bible teaches that a remnant of the Jews will one day accept Jesus as their Messiah (Zech. 12:10 and Rom. 9:27). As I have pointed out repeatedly, this will occur at the end of the Tribulation when Jesus returns to this earth. He will gather the believing Jewish remnant to the land of Israel, and they will be established as the foremost nation in the world (Ezek. 37:11–28 and Zech. 8:22–23). Jesus will then rule over the house of Jacob.

The current Church kingdom is not an everlasting kingdom. The Church Age kingdom will end with the Rapture of the Church. The Church kingdom will be followed by the millennial kingdom, and that kingdom will be followed by the final, eternal kingdom of Christ that will be established on a new, perfected earth (1 Cor. 15:24 and Rev. 21:1–8).

Believing God's Word

Why can't we accept the promises made to Mary to mean what they say? The first four meant exactly what they said. Why must the last three be spiritualized? The only reason for spiritualizing them is to force them to conform to some preconceived system.

I believe God knows how to communicate. If God had intended to promise Mary that her son would reign from heaven over the Church forever, He would have said so. Instead, He reaffirmed to her the promise He had made many times through the Old Testament prophets that His Son would reign from David's throne in Jerusalem over Israel and that He would be given a kingdom that would last forever (Isa. 9:6–7 and Ezek. 37:21–28).

If the promises God made to the Jews did not mean what they said, then how can we be sure that His promises to the Church mean what they say? I believe God means what He says.

Our Hope

Just as He fulfilled all the promises related to the first coming of His Son, God is going to fulfill all those that relate to His second coming, including the promise of a millennial reign. Many in the Church may be ignorant of His unfulfilled promises. Others may have forgotten them. But God has not. He intends to fulfill every one of them. We are privileged to live in a time when we can witness God orchestrating the events of this world to the fulfillment of all the promises in His master plan.

Ascribe greatness to our God! The Rock! His work is perfect, For all His ways are just; A God of faithfulness and without injustice, Righteous and upright is He (Deut. 32:3–4).

Chapter 4

Probing Revelation

I s going to hell something like being sucked into a black hole in space?"

"I'm pregnant, and I want to know, if the Rapture were to occur today, would the baby in my womb go to heaven with me?"

"I've heard that Prince Charles of England has a name that adds up to 666 and that his coat of arms contains symbols from the Book of Daniel. Could he really be the Antichrist?"

"I've heard there are Russian troops stationed in the United States and that they fly around the country in black helicopters. Could this be the invasion of locusts portrayed in Revelation 9?"

Challenging Questions

I've been conducting Bible conferences about Revelation for the past 20 years all across the United States and around the world. My favorite part is when I open the conference to questions, and I think that the participants also enjoy it the most.

Some of the questions are bizarre. Some are funny. Some are difficult and challenging. But I find it enjoyable to respond to all of them.

Sometimes I have to respond by saying, "I don't know." Other times I have to explain that there are several possible answers and that no one really knows which answer is correct. Often, members of the audience will help me with the answers.

One memorable occasion occurred when I was asked, "What language will we speak in heaven?" I responded by saying I thought it would be Hebrew, and I provided some biblical reasons for thinking so.

When I finished elaborating on my answer, an Hispanic man stood up and said, "Sir, I would like to respectfully disagree with you. I think our heavenly language will be Spanish."

"Why do you think that?" I asked.

"Because it is the most beautiful of all languages," he responded.

I told him I could agree with that observation, but I said I needed some biblical evidence for his answer.

He replied with a big smile, "Haven't you ever heard of the Chicano glory of God?"

The audience erupted in laughter. I replied that I had heard about the Lord's Shekinah glory, but I wasn't sure about any Chicano glory!

Years later when I shared this story with a colleague, Arno Frose of Midnight Call Ministries, he responded in his German accent, "Both of you are wrong!"

"Oh?" I said. "What language do you think it will be?"

"German!" He snapped.

"Do you have any biblical basis for that conclusion?" I asked.

"Yes, I do," he replied. "In 2 Corinthians 12 it says that Paul was taken up to heaven and that he heard things there that were 'inexpressible.' Doesn't that sound like German to you?"

I had to agree, but I sure hope he is wrong!

A Tough Polish Question

One of the funniest things that ever happened to me in a question and answer session occurred in a conference in Warsaw, Poland. Another colleague of mine, Gary Fisher of Lion of Judah Ministries, was conducting the session with me.

Gary was holding the microphone when a very intense lady got up and asked a long and technical question. By the time it was translated into English, it was indecipherable.

Gary thought about the question for a moment, and then he said, "Lady, your question reminds me of a story I heard recently about a nuclear physicist in the United States. He was invited to make a tour of universities to speak about nuclear development and applications. He was afraid of flying, so he hired a car and chauffeur.

"After the fifth delivery of his speech, while he was en route to his next engagement, the chauffeur suddenly said, 'Sir, I've heard you give that speech five times. I think I now know it by heart. And you know what? I think I could deliver it better than you can!'

"'Okay, wise guy,' the physicist replied, 'let's put you to the test. At our next university let's switch clothes, and you deliver the speech.'

"So, at the next stop that's what they did, and the chauffeur proceeded to prove his point. He delivered the speech flawlessly and eloquently. But he got so carried away with himself that he made the mistake of calling for questions from the audience.

"The first question was a torturous one. The chauffeur thought about it for a moment and then replied, 'That is the stupidest question I have heard in a long time. It is so simplistic, in fact, that my chauffeur could answer it!' At that point he handed the microphone to his chauffeur."

And at that same moment, my "friend," Gary Fisher, handed me the mike and said, "Answer the lady's question." They say jokes don't translate, but that one did. It brought down the house!

Frequently Asked Questions

Well, let's proceed to consider some of the most frequently asked questions related to the Book of Revelation. Remember, I don't claim to have all the answers. In fact, I have a list of my own questions that I am anxious to ask the Lord when I stand face to face with Him. Until then, all of us are going to be limited to some degree in our understanding by the fact that "we see in a mirror dimly" (1 Cor. 13:12).

I will not cover all the frequently asked questions because many of them have already been dealt with in chapter 2 in my overview of the Book of Revelation. I will deal here with the matters I skipped in that overview or the significant ones I mentioned only briefly in passing.

I also intend to deal only with major issues and not with the dozens of questions that could be asked about matters that are not highly significant — like: Who are the "Nicolaitans"? (Rev. 2:6). Who are those "who say they are Jews, and are not"? (Rev. 2:9 and 3:9). Who is "the woman Jezebel, who calls herself a prophetess"? (Rev. 2:20).

I will also deal with some questions about Revelation that have arisen from the immensely popular "Left Behind" series of books that are being written by Tim LaHaye and Jerry Jenkins. This series presents the story of the Tribulation in fictionalized form.

Keep in mind that the Bible does not reveal everything about the future. But it reveals enough to give us hope and great expectations. I suggest that you not fret over the things you do not understand. Rather, rejoice over those promises that are clear. Don't give up on the points you don't understand. Pray about them and keep searching the Scriptures, but don't allow them to destroy the peace you should have about those aspects of the future that the Bible clearly reveals.

Is Revelation prophecy or history?

The book itself declares that it is prophecy: "Blessed is he who reads and those who hear the words of the prophecy" (Rev. 1:3). Four additional times in the last chapter of the book the message is declared to be prophetic (Rev. 22:7, 10, 18, and 19).

So, the real question should be, "Is Revelation fulfilled prophecy?" I have already spoken to this issue elsewhere in this book, so I will not go into detail. Suffice it for me to say that everything in the book from chapter 4 on is yet future. The future aspects are introduced in chapter 4 verse 1 where John is raptured to heaven and is informed that he will be shown "what must take place after these things."

Those who argue that the prophecies of Revelation have been fulfilled in history can do so only by spiritualizing the book. Where in history was one-fourth of humanity killed in one war? (Rev. 6:1–8). Where is the historical record of 144,000 Jews being suddenly saved and then called for special service in the Lord's kingdom? (Rev. 7:1–8). Has there ever been a war that resulted in the slaughter of one-third of humanity? (Rev. 8 and 9). Has there ever been a locust invasion, real or symbolic, that resulted in all unsaved people suffering terrible torment for five months while saved people experienced immunity? (Rev. 9:1–11). Where in history are the two witnesses of Revelation 11 or the two beasts of Revelation 13?

I could go on and on, but I think the point has been made. The prophecies of Revelation await fulfillment.

Was Revelation written before or after the fall of Jerusalem?

The internal evidence of the book regarding the Roman Empire and the external testimony of the Church Fathers both point to a date of authorship around A.D. 95, 25 years after the destruction of Jerusalem in A.D. 70.

The type of widespread Roman persecution of the Church that is pictured in Revelation did not occur until the reign of Domitian (A.D. 81–96). The persecutions of Nero were limited to the area of Rome. One of the Church Fathers, Irenaeus (c. 130–c. 202), wrote that the Book of Revelation was authored by the apostle John "toward the end of Domitian's reign."[1] Irenaeus was discipled by Polycarp (A.D. c. 70–c. 155) who, in turn, had been discipled directly by John himself.

One of the arguments for an earlier date is based on a reference to the temple in Revelation 11:1–2. John is told to measure the temple, which in this case seems to be a command to assess the temple's spiritual condition. This reference to the temple, it is argued, must mean that the book was written before the temple was destroyed in A.D. 70.

But this argument ignores the fact that the Scriptures teach that there are going to be two future temples, one during the Tribulation which the Antichrist will desecrate (Dan. 9:27 and 2 Thess. 2:3–4), and another during the Millennium which Jesus Christ will consecrate (Ezek. 40–46).

The temple mentioned in Revelation 11 must be the Tribulation temple since the passage says it will be trampled down by the Gentiles for 42 months (the last half of the Tribulation). It also says this will be immediately preceded by the testimony of the two witnesses for 1,260 days (the first half of the Tribulation).

Doesn't the Book of Revelation infer that its prophecies were to be fulfilled in the time it was written?

It would be easy to get this impression because the very first verse speaks of "the things which must shortly take place" (Rev. 1:1). Also, two times the text states that "the time is near" for the fulfillment of the prophecies (Rev. 1:3 and 22:10).

But in view of the fact that the prophecies have not been literally fulfilled in history, it appears that these statements point to imminence rather than nearness in time. Imminence is the concept that an event can occur at any time, and the creation of that sense seems to be the purpose of these statements.

The principle is one that Jesus stressed in His teachings about the end times. Over and over He told His disciples to be ready for His return at any moment. "Be ready," He warned, "for the Son of Man is coming at an hour when you do not think He will" (Matt. 24:44). Jesus used the parable of the ten virgins to illustrate His point. Five were unready when the bridegroom came and were thus left behind. "Be on the alert, then," Jesus warned, "for you do not know the day nor the hour" (Matt. 25:1–13). On another occasion, He put it this way, "Be dressed in readiness, and keep your lamps alight. . . . for the Son of Man is coming at an hour that you do not expect" (Luke 12:35–40).

The apostolic writers make it clear that living in a state of suspense, expecting the Lord to return shortly, at any moment, will have a purifying effect, because it will motivate holiness. Paul urges us to "deny ungodliness and worldly desires and to live sensibly, righteously and godly in the present age, looking for the blessed hope and appearing of the glory of our great God and Savior, Christ Jesus" (Titus 2:12–13). Peter tells each of us to "keep sober in spirit," and he says the way to do it is to "fix your hope completely on the grace to be brought to you at the revelation of Jesus Christ" (1 Pet. 1:13). John says we are to focus on the Lord's return because "everyone who has this hope fixed on Him purifies himself just as He is" (1 John 3:3).

Words must always be interpreted in terms of context, and context is often shaped by historical setting. In the first century setting, the references to "soon," "shortly," and "near" seemed to indicate a quick fulfillment. But as time has passed without any literal fulfillment, history has shaped the context to indicate imminence — that is, the events prophesied can happen any moment.

A similar phenomenon can be found in statements used in other portions of the Scriptures. For example, James wrote that we are to be patient until the coming of the Lord, and then he stated, "the coming of the Lord is at hand . . . behold, the Judge is standing right at the door" (James 5:7-9). In like manner, Peter wrote, "The end of all things is at hand" (1 Pet. 4:7). The fact of the matter is that we have been living in the end times ever since the Day of Pentecost when the gospel was first preached, and the end times could be consummated any moment with the fulfillment of Revelation's prophecies.

The generalized time references in Revelation are not indicators of nearness in time. Instead, they are warnings of imminence — that the events prophesied could start unfolding at any moment.

Are the 144,000 really Jews?

There is probably no part of Revelation that has been more abused than the first half of chapter 7 which tells about 144,000 Jews being "sealed" as "bond-servants" of God. The Jehovah's Witnesses claim that a group of their founders and pioneers constitute this group. Other cults claim they are the 144,000. Most mainline Christian commentators argue that this group is symbolic of the Church.

How 144,000 Jews could be symbolic of the Church is beyond my comprehension. This interpretation is a good example of the fanciful ideas that people seem to delight in pulling out of Revelation. What would God have to do to convince us that He is speaking about 144,000 Jews? He says they are Jews. Specifically, He calls them, "the sons of Israel" (Rev. 7:4). He even enumerates them by their tribes, stating that 12,000 will come from each tribe. Does He need to put a flashing neon sign in the sky that says, "I'm talking about Jews!"?

Why are some Jewish tribes excluded from the 144,000?

This is an intriguing question. The list of tribes is certainly unusual. The original 12 tribes included both Levi and Joseph. But normally, when the 12 tribes are listed in the Bible, Levi — the priestly tribe — is not mentioned because its inheritance was the Lord himself (Deut. 10:9). And Joseph's name is usually dropped and then replaced by his two sons, Ephraim and Manasseh who were adopted by Jacob (Gen. 48:8–22). So, Levi and Joseph are usually replaced by Ephraim and Manasseh, keeping the list at 12.

In the listing in Revelation 7, the tribes of Dan and Ephraim are dropped and replaced by Levi and Joseph to keep the list at 12. Why? Well, no one knows for sure. My guess is that Dan and Ephraim were dropped because they were the ones that led the Children of Israel into idolatry (Deut. 29:18–21 and 1 Kings 12:25–33). It thus appears that the two tribes responsible for luring others into idolatry will not be entrusted with sharing the gospel with others during the Tribulation.

But God's grace in this matter is reflected at the end of Revelation when the description of the New Jerusalem is given. Revelation 21:12 says the city will have 12 gates and that each gate will be named after one of "the twelve tribes of the sons of Israel." In Ezekiel 48:30–34 we are told which tribes will be included in this significant recognition. They are the original 12, including Levi and Joseph. That means one of the gates will be named for the errant tribe of Dan, and both Manessah and Ephraim will be included under Joseph's name.

Are the 144,000 of Revelation 7 the same as the 144,000 portrayed in Revelation 14?

I believe they are. Why would the book introduce us to a totally different group of 144,000 people without telling us so?

In his book, *Revelation Illustrated and Made Plain*, Tim LaHaye argues that the 144,000 in Revelation 14 are a group of Gentile Christians who have been converted during the Tribulation and who have served the Lord with distinction before experiencing martyrdom. He admits that this interpretation puts him "in the minority among commentators."[2]

The scene in Revelation 14 portrays 144,000 men standing on Mount Zion with Jesus. LaHaye contends that since this scene takes place in the middle of the Tribulation, and since Jesus would not be standing on Mount Zion in Jerusalem at that time, the reference to Mount Zion must be a symbolic reference to heaven. So, he concludes that these are Gentiles who have died for their faith and who are now in heaven with Jesus.

I don't think so. The first point I would make is that this scene is not in the middle of the Tribulation. All of chapter 14 is a flash-forward to the end of the Tribulation, giving the reader a preview of what lies ahead, assuring him that Jesus will ultimately triumph. The second point I would make is that the group is not in heaven. They are on Mount Zion in Jerusalem where Jesus has returned to reign as King of kings.

He has preserved them through the Tribulation, and He is celebrating His victory with them. They are singing a song heard from heaven, a song which only they can sing (Rev. 14:2–3). Again, if this were a different 144,000 from the 144,000 Jews mentioned in Revelation 7, I think the text would tell us so.

Why does God seem to be so obsessed with the Jews?

This is a frequent question during prophetic forums. The answer is that He loves them, just like He loves all His creation. But there is certainly a sense in which Bible prophecy seems to focus upon the Jewish people. That's because God called the Jews to be His "chosen people" through whom He would accomplish His master plan for history (Deut. 7:6). It was through the Jewish people that God gave the world His Word. And it was through the Jews that He sent the Messiah.

The Hebrew Scriptures say that the Jews were also chosen to be witnesses of God — of what it means to have a relationship with Him (Isa. 43:10–12). The history of Israel attests to the fact that when one is faithful to God, He blesses; when one is unfaithful, He disciplines; and when one repents, God forgives and forgets and begins to bless once again. Currently, the Jews are under God's discipline, but Bible prophecy tells us a day is coming when a great remnant of them will repent and receive Jesus as their Messiah (Zech. 12:10). When that happens, God will make them the most exalted nation in the world (Isa. 60 through 61:5). Jesus will live among them as King of kings (Ezek. 43:7), and all of God's blessings to the nations will flow through them (Zech. 8:22–23).

The Jews are also God's prophetic time clock. By this, I mean He often relates major future events to things that will happen to the Jews as a nation. Daniel's prophecy of the 70 weeks of years is a good example. Daniel says to watch for a decree that will allow the rebuilding of Jerusalem. He then states that 483 years after that decree is issued, the Messiah will come and die (Dan. 9:24–26).

In the New Testament, we have another good example. Jesus told His disciples that a day would come when the Jews would be dispersed among all the nations of the world and Jerusalem would be trampled down by the Gentiles. But then He added that when Jerusalem is no longer under Gentile control, He would return (Luke 21:24). Jesus was simply emphasizing a point that is made repeatedly in the Hebrew Scriptures — namely, that when the Jews are restored to their land, to the city of Jerusalem, the Messiah will come (Zech. 12:3, 6, 8–10, and 13:1).

Another reason for the prophetic focus upon the Jews is because God has promised that He will bring a great remnant to salvation during the final years of Daniel's 70 weeks of years. The Bible makes it clear that during the last half of the Tribulation, God will focus the wrath of the Antichrist upon the Jews, bringing them to the end of themselves and motivating them to turn to God in repentance (Zech. 12:10, Rom. 9:27 and 11:25–26).

Hasn't the disobedience of the Jews invalidated God's promises to them?

Absolutely not. Or, to put it in the words of the apostle Paul, "May it never be!" (Rom. 11:1).

Ever since the fourth century, when the Church adopted amillennialism and began to divorce itself from its Jewish heritage, the prevalent Christian view concerning the Jews has been that "God washed His hands of them" in the first century when He poured out His wrath on Jerusalem and allowed the Jews to be dispersed worldwide. An accompanying doctrine that developed over the years is called "replacement theology." It is the idea that God replaced the Jews with the Church, that the Church has become the "new Israel," and that the Church has inherited all the blessings that were previously promised to the Jews. Needless to say, these ideas have served as a source of much of the anti-Semitism that has characterized the Church for the past 1,600 years.

The idea that God has "washed His hands of the Jews" is thoroughly unbiblical. In Jeremiah 31:36 God says the Jewish people will continue to be "a nation before Me forever."

He emphasizes the point by saying they will continue as a special nation of people until the fixed order of the universe ceases, or until all the heavens and ocean depths have been measured (Jer. 31:36–37). In Isaiah 49:14–16 God uses a different metaphor to emphasize His devotion to Israel. He says that He has the nation inscribed on the palms of His hands!

There are three chapters in the New Testament that strongly emphasize the continuing love of God for the Jews. These three chapters have been despised and ignored (or spiritualized into meaninglessness) throughout much of Christian history. The chapters are Romans 9–11. In Romans 9:4 Paul writes that God still has covenants with the Jews which He promises to fulfill. He then makes it clear that the Jews who will receive the blessings are a great remnant that will be saved in the end times (Rom. 9:27).

Paul even specifically addresses the question of whether or not God has rejected the Jewish people. He asks, "God has not rejected His people has He?" (Rom. 11:1). For 1,600 years the Church has answered this question with an unqualified, "Yes!" But Paul answers it by saying, "May it never be! . . . God has not rejected His people whom He foreknew" (Rom. 11:1–2).

But what about their disobedience? What about their rejection of God as king of their nation and Jesus as king of their hearts? Hasn't their disobedience nullified the promises of God? Again, Paul specifically deals with this issue. He asks, "What then? If some did not believe, their unbelief will not nullify the faithfulness of God, will it?" (Rom. 3:3). And again, for centuries the Church has responded, "Yes!" But not Paul. He responds by saying, "May it never be! Rather, let God be found true, though every man be found a liar" (Rom. 3:4).

Paul becomes so overwhelmed by the grace of God in never giving up on the Jews, that he finally bursts forth with an ecstatic proclamation: "Oh, the depth of the riches both of the wisdom and knowledge of God! How unsearchable are His judgments and unfathomable His ways!" (Rom. 11:33).

When I first started preaching about God's love for the

Jewish people and His absolute determination to bring a great remnant to salvation despite their stubbornness and rebellion, my wife said, "You make me want to be a Jew!" I responded by saying, "No, dear, you wouldn't want to be a Jew because the overwhelming odds are that you would have a spiritual veil that would keep you from recognizing Jesus as your Messiah" (2 Cor. 3:14–16).

I then pointed out to her that God is not doing one thing for the Jewish people that He is not willing to do for anyone. The Jews, again, are simply a witness of God's desire for all people to come to repentance and be saved (2 Pet. 3:9). God does not "wash His hands" of anyone. He pursues and pursues, trying to bring us to the end of ourselves so that we will turn to Him in repentance and be saved. That is exactly what is going to happen to the Jewish remnant at the end of the Tribulation. Here's how the prophet Malachi put it:

> Who can endure the day of His coming? And who can stand when He appears? For He is like a refiner's fire and like fullers' soap. And He will sit as a smelter and purifier of silver, and He will purify the sons of Levi and refine them like gold and silver, so that they may present to the Lord offerings in righteousness. Then the offering of Judah and Jerusalem will be pleasing to the Lord, as in the days of old and as in former years (Mal. 3:2–4).

Is the return of the Lord really going to be in stages?

Yes, the concept of the Lord returning in stages is very biblical and can be proved rather easily. The New Testament contains only two detailed descriptions of the Lord's return. One is found in 1 Thessalonians 4:13–18, and the other in Revelation 19:11–16. When the two are compared, it becomes very evident that the only thing they have in common is that they both focus on Jesus. Otherwise, they are as different as night and day. Consider the differences:

1 Thessalonians 4	Revelation 19
Jesus appears in the heavens.	Jesus returns to earth.
He appears for His church.	He returns with His church.
He appears as a bridegroom.	He returns as a warrior.
He appears to claim the righteous.	He returns to condemn the unrighteous.
He appears as a deliverer.	He returns as King of kings.

These two passages are obviously talking about two different events. The passage in 1 Thessalonians 4 describes what has come to be known as the Rapture — the snatching of the Church out of the world. Revelation 19 describes an event that will take place later — the return of the Lord to the earth.

In other words, the second coming of Jesus is going to be in two stages. First, He will appear in the heavens for His church, claiming the redeemed from the earth and taking them back to heaven. Then, later, He will return with His church to reign on the earth.

This method of reconciling these two passages solves a serious problem that emerges when you think of only one future coming of the Lord. That problem relates to the emphasis that the Scriptures give to imminence. As I have indicated repeatedly, the Scriptures warn that the Lord may appear at any moment and, therefore, we are always to be ready for His return. (See, for example, Matt. 24:36, 42, 44 and 25:13.)

If there is only one future coming of the Lord, then these warnings are a waste of time, and there is no imminence because there are many prophecies that are yet to be fulfilled before the Lord can return. I have in mind such things as a peace treaty that will bring true peace to Israel and enable the Jews to rebuild their temple (Dan. 9:27). Also, there must be a seven-year period of Tribulation during which the Antichrist will terrorize the world (Rev. 6-18).

These are just a few of the events that are clearly prophesied in Scripture as occurring before Jesus returns to earth. If there is only one future coming of the Lord, and it must take place after these events, then the Lord's return is not imminent. We should not be living looking for Jesus Christ, as the Scriptures instruct us to do (Titus 2:13). Rather, we should be looking for the Antichrist.

The only way there can be imminence is for there to be two future comings of the Lord, one of which — the Rapture — can occur any moment. And the Rapture truly is imminent because there is not one prophecy that must be fulfilled for it to occur. It is an event that could happen any moment.

You say Jesus can come at any moment, but doesn't the Bible say that the gospel must be preached to all the world before Jesus can return?

Yes, the Bible does say that all the world must hear the gospel before Jesus will return. In fact, Jesus himself was the one who said this. It is recorded in His Olivet Discourse: "And this gospel of the kingdom shall be preached in the whole world for a witness to all the nations, and then the end shall come" (Matt. 24:14).

But this statement relates to His return to this earth at His second coming. It does not relate to the Rapture when He will appear in the heavens for His church. During the Tribulation there is going to be much preaching of the gospel. The 144,000 Jews who will be sealed at the beginning of the Tribulation will serve as "servants" of God (Rev. 7:3). Any true servant of God is one who shares the message of the gospel with others. The gospel will also be proclaimed by the two witnesses in Jerusalem (Rev. 11:1-7). Those converted to Jesus during the Tribulation, both Jew and Gentile, will share the gospel with others. At the end of the Tribulation, right before the pouring out of the bowls of wrath, God in His grace and mercy is going to send an angel who will circumnavigate the globe preaching the "eternal gospel" to "every nation and tribe and tongue and people" (Rev. 14:6). The preaching of this gospel angel will serve to fulfill Jesus' prophecy.

Does the Rapture mark the beginning of the Tribulation?

No, the Bible does not state anywhere that the Tribulation begins with the Rapture. I believe the Rapture could occur months or even years before the Tribulation begins, although it is likely to occur near the beginning because the Tribulation is the time of the pouring out of God's wrath, and 1 Thessalonians 1:10 says that Jesus will "deliver" His church "from the wrath to come."

Another reason for believing the Rapture is likely to occur near the beginning of the Tribulation is because 2 Thessalonians 2 says that the Antichrist cannot be revealed until a "restrainer" is "taken out of the way" (2 Thess. 2:6–7). I believe that restrainer is the Holy Spirit working through the Church. Thus, when the Church is removed, the Antichrist will be unleashed, and the Tribulation will begin.

The prophet Daniel indicates that the starting point of the Tribulation will be a "covenant" that the Antichrist will arrange for Israel that will evidently guarantee the nation's peace and enable the Jews to rebuild their temple (Dan. 9:27).

Why isn't the Rapture specifically mentioned in Revelation?

As I mentioned earlier in chapter 2, the Book of Revelation implies a pre-Tribulation Rapture without specifically mentioning the event. In chapter 4 verse 1, John sees a door open in the heavens and he is raptured to heaven in what appears to be a symbolic type of the Rapture of the Church. In Revelation 19:11, John sees the heavens opened again, and Jesus descends on a white horse, with the Church accompanying Him (Rev. 19:14). Chapters 2 and 3 of Revelation focus on the Church, but there is no more mention of the Church until the end of the book (Rev. 22:16). From chapter 4 through chapter 21, there is only mention of "saints," which would be those who accept the gospel during the Tribulation.

The Bible never specifically defines the timing of the Rapture by tying it to any other event like the re-establishment of Israel or the re-building of the temple. Even its proximity to the Tribulation is inferred rather than definitely stated. That's because the Rapture is an imminent event that could occur at any moment.

There are strong scriptural inferences that the Rapture will occur before the Tribulation begins. A couple of those are found in Jesus' Olivet Discourse as recorded in Luke 21. Jesus stated that when the end-time signs "begin to take place," we are to look up, for our redemption will be drawing near (Luke 21:28). Note that the redemption will come not at the end of the signs, but as they *begin* to take place. Jesus then added that believers should pray earnestly that they might "escape" the great tribulation that is coming upon "all those who dwell on the face of the earth" (Luke 21:36).

In this regard, Paul states in 1 Thessalonians 1:10 that believers are waiting for "His Son from heaven . . . that is, Jesus, who delivers us from the wrath to come." And Jesus told John to write to the church at Philadelphia, representative of faithful Christians, that "because you have kept the word of My perseverance, I also will keep you from the hour of testing, that hour which is about to come upon the whole world, to test those who dwell upon the earth" (Rev. 3:10).

Isn't a mid-Tribulation Rapture inferred in Revelation?

Some people think so. They point first to 1 Corinthians 15:51–52, which says the Rapture will occur at the blowing of the "last trumpet." They then point to Revelation 11:15 where the seventh and last trumpet of the trumpet judgments is blown. Since this seventh trumpet appears to be blown in the middle of the Tribulation, after the Antichrist kills the two witnesses, the argument is that this must mark the time of the Rapture.

There are several problems with this argument. In the first place, there is nothing in the Bible that identifies the seventh trumpet of the trumpet judgments in Revelation as the "last trumpet" of 1 Corinthians 15. The assumption that the two are the same is just that — an assumption. It is a shaky assumption because the trumpets of Revelation are announcing judgments that are aimed at unbelievers. They don't have any relationship to believers.

Now, there is a trumpet that the "last trumpet" of 1 Corinthians 15:32 can be identified with. It is the "trumpet of God" which 1 Thessalonians 4:16 says will be blown when the Rapture occurs. With that in mind, consider the fact that the last trumpet of the trumpet judgments in Revelation 11:15 is not identified as the trumpet of God but as the trumpet of an angel.

The second problem with the mid-Tribulation Rapture concept is that the seventh trumpet of Revelation 11 really doesn't relate to the middle of the Tribulation at all. Its blowing triggers a flash-forward to the end of the Tribulation to the proclamation that "the kingdom of the world has become the kingdom of our Lord, and of His Christ, and He will reign forever and ever" (Rev. 11:15).

Another thing to consider is that 1 Corinthians 15 was written about 45 years before the Book of Revelation. Thus, it seems logical that the reference to a "last trumpet" must refer to something in the Old Testament that the Corinthian church would have been familiar with. That would most likely have been the trumpet referred to by both Joel and Zephaniah — the trumpet that will be blown *before* the Day of the Lord's judgment (Joel 2:1 and Zeph. 1:16).

Can an argument be made for placing the Rapture near the end of the Tribulation?

Some have tried to do this, arguing that the wrath of God is not poured out until the end of the Tribulation. This concept is called the "pre-wrath Rapture."[3]

The cornerstone of this concept is that the terrifying events during the first half of the Tribulation are due to the wrath of man and Satan, and not to God. Since the Church is only promised protection from the wrath of God, the Rapture will not occur until near the end of the Tribulation when God will pour out His wrath on the world.

This concept raises a serious theological problem because it questions the sovereignty of God. It assumes that man and Satan can act apart from God's will, when the fact of the matter is that neither can do anything God is not willing to permit. The Bible often portrays God carrying out His will through evil persons or nations. One of the classic examples is when He allowed the evil nation of Babylon to discipline Israel by destroying Jerusalem and the temple and by carrying the surviving Jews away into captivity. It was an action that prompted the prophet Habakkuk to ask why God would punish those who are evil with those who are more evil (Hab. 1:13).

Any carnage wrought by man or Satan during the Tribulation will still constitute the wrath of God. They will simply be His instruments. The Bible says God sits in the heavens and laughs over the plots and deeds of evil men, not because He does not care, but because He has everything under control (Ps. 2:1–6). The point is that He has the wisdom and power to orchestrate all evil to the triumph of His will in history. That's why the Psalmist wrote that "the wrath of man shall praise You [God]" (Ps. 76:10).

I think it is also important to note that when God pours out His wrath, He does not always do so directly. One of His most common ways is to simply back away from the nation or person and lower the hedge of protection around them. This is clearly spelled out in Romans 1:18–32. That passage says that when people rebel against God to the point that they begin to worship the creation rather than the Creator, God "gives them over" to the evil in their hearts. In other words, He just steps back and lets evil multiply. The passage further states that if they still refuse to repent, He steps back again and "gives them over to degrading passions." And if they persist in their rebellion and sin, He finally "gives them over to a depraved mind" at which point the society destroys itself. Such destruction could be viewed as the wrath of man, but it is really the wrath of God working through man.

There is another serious problem with the pre-wrath Rapture concept. It relates to the fact that all the wrath of Revelation is specifically portrayed as the wrath of God. Where do the seal judgments originate? The answer is from the throne of God as Jesus opens each seal of the scroll that was in the Father's right hand (Rev. 6:1). And where do the trumpet judgments originate? The same place — from the throne of God (Rev. 8:2). When we arrive at the bowl judgments in Revelation 15:1, we are told that with them, "the wrath of God is finished."

Another problem with the pre-wrath concept is that it does violence to the chronological order of Revelation. The seal judgments are viewed as the wrath of man and Satan, occurring during the first half of the Tribulation. The trumpet and bowl judgments are considered to be the wrath of God. They are lumped together at the end of the Tribulation. There is no justification for putting the trumpet judgments at the end of the Tribulation. They are clearly placed in the first half of the Tribulation in the chronological layout of the Book of Revelation.

One final problem with the pre-wrath concept of the Rapture is that it disputes the fact that there is no purpose for the Church being in the Tribulation. The Tribulation is the 70th week of Daniel, a time devoted to God accomplishing His purposes among the Jewish people, not the Church.

Couldn't God just protect believers during the Tribulation? Is it really necessary to remove them from the earth?

Yes, the Lord could provide believers with supernatural protection. In fact, He will do precisely that when He provides saints who are present in the Tribulation with protection from the stings of the demonic locust attack that will be part of the trumpet judgments (Rev. 9:4).

But God's promise to the Church during the Tribulation is not one of protection, but one of deliverance. Jesus said that when the signs pointing to the Tribulation "begin to take place," believers are to look up because their "redemption is drawing near" (Luke 21:28). He also urged believers to pray that they might "escape all these things" (Luke 21:36).

There really is no purpose for the Church to be present during the Tribulation. It is a time of the pouring out of God's wrath upon those who have rejected His grace, love, and mercy. There are some who argue that the Church must be "purged" during the Tribulation to purify it. But to me, this idea is absurd. The blood of Jesus is sufficient to cleanse us of all our sins. That is an accomplished fact for those who have put their faith in Jesus (Eph. 5:26–27). Furthermore, the concept of purging the Church during the Tribulation converts the whole period into a Protestant version of purgatory. It also violates the wedding imagery that the Bible uses to describe the relationship between Christ and His church. Jesus is not going to beat up His bride for seven years and then marry her!

Some who believe that the Church will go through the Tribulation often point to the example of Noah and his family. They were left on the earth as God poured out His wrath, but they were protected by the Lord. But this example ignores the fact that Enoch was raptured out of the world before the flood began (Gen. 5:24). I believe Enoch is a symbolic type of the Church and Noah and his family are a type of the Jewish remnant that will be protected through the Tribulation until the day that the Messiah returns.

Aren't those of you who believe in a Pre-Tribulation Rapture a bunch of escapists who are not willing to suffer for the Lord?

There is nothing wrong with being an "escapist." Noah was an escapist and so was Lot. And Jesus said that when the end-time signs begin to appear, we are to pray "to escape the things that are about to take place and to stand before the Son of Man" (Luke 21:36).

Certainly we are called to suffer for Christ (Rom. 8:17). And anyone who truly stands for Jesus in this world will be persecuted (John 15:19). We are assured that as believers we will suffer tribulation in this world (John 16:33), but we are

promised that we will be exempted from the great tribulation
that will one day come upon all the world (Rev. 3:10).

Will children be taken in the Rapture?

This is one of the most frequently asked questions. The
"Left Behind" series answers this question with a resounding
"Yes!"[4] I hope that answer is correct.

The problem is that the Bible does not clearly answer the
question. Nowhere does it state that children will be raptured.
Tim LaHaye presents his theological reasoning for his con-
viction in the words of a pastor who is raptured but who leaves
behind a video tape for those who miss the Rapture:

> Up to a certain age, which is probably differ-
> ent for each individual, we believe God will not hold
> a child accountable for a decision that must be made
> with heart and mind, fully cognizant of the ramifi-
> cations. You may also find that unborn children have
> disappeared from their mother's wombs.[5]

I think a strong argument can be made that the minor
children of *believers* will be taken in the Rapture. That argument would be based in part on the fact that God saved Noah
and all his household when He destroyed the earth with water. Likewise, God saved Lot and his two daughters when He
decided to destroy Sodom and Gomorrah (2 Pet. 2:4–9). Ad-
ditionally, there is an interesting verse in 1 Corinthians 7:14
that may be applicable here: "The Christian wife brings holiness to her marriage, and the Christian husband brings holiness to his marriage. Otherwise, your children would not have
a godly influence, but now they are set apart" (NLT).[6] A principle stated in Proverbs 14:26 may also be applicable: "Those
who fear the Lord are secure; He will be a place of refuge for
their children" (NLT).

I certainly would agree that children who die before the
age of accountability are saved. King David recognized this
when his baby born of Bathsheba died (2 Sam. 12:23). And
Jesus said, "Truly I say to you, unless you are converted and

become like children, you shall not enter the kingdom of heaven" (Matt. 18:3).

But the Rapture is a promise to the Church, and minor children who have not accepted the Lord are not members of the Church.

The fact that the Rapture is a promise to the Church, and the Church alone, is often overlooked. Many people assume that all saved people who have ever lived will be resurrected at the time of the Rapture. That is not so. The Bible makes it clear that Old Testament saints will be resurrected at the end of the Tribulation (Dan. 12:1–2).

So, to summarize, the "Left Behind" series may be right in its assumption that all children will be raptured. Again, I hope it is, but the Bible is silent on the issue. If any children are raptured, they are more likely to be the children of believers.

Can people still be saved after the Rapture?

There is no doubt that there will be a great harvest of souls after the Rapture (Rev. 7:9–14). Some will be convicted by the Rapture itself. Others will be converted by the preaching of either the two witnesses in Jerusalem (Rev. 11) or the 144,000 Jewish disciples who will serve as servants of God (Rev. 7). Some will repent in response to the judgments of God (Isa. 26:9). Others will respond to an angel of God who will preach the "eternal gospel" to all the world at the end of the Tribulation, right before the final pouring out of God's wrath (Rev. 14:6).

The controversial issue is whether or not those who have heard the gospel before the Rapture and have rejected it will be allowed to respond and be saved after the Rapture. The "Left Behind" series takes the position that such people will be able to accept Jesus as Lord and Savior after the Rapture.[7]

But not all prophecy teachers would agree. The reason for the controversy is a passage in 2 Thessalonians 2:8–12 which seems to indicate that such people will continue to reject the gospel after the Rapture. Here's the passage. Read it for yourself and draw your own conclusion:

And then that lawless one will be revealed
whom the Lord will slay with the breath of His
mouth and bring to an end by the appearance of
His coming; that is, the one whose coming is in ac-
cord with the activity of Satan, with all power and
signs and false wonders, and with all the deception
of wickedness for those who perish, because they
did not receive the love of the truth so as to be saved.
For this reason God will send upon them a delud-
ing influence so that they will believe what is false,
in order that they all may be judged who did not
believe the truth, but took pleasure in wickedness.

This passage seems to teach that people who have rejected
the truth before the Rapture will continue to do so. Because of
this passage, I cannot say with absolute confidence that those
who have rejected the gospel before the Rapture will have the
possibility of accepting it afterwards. I hope Tim LaHaye is
right, but I would not want to give such people any false hope.

Revelation speaks about two resurrections. Doesn't your end-time system contain more than two resurrections?

Yes, Revelation does speak of two resurrections (Rev.
20:4, 12). Elsewhere, the Bible speaks of "a resurrection of
life" and "a resurrection of judgment" (John 5:29). In Acts
24:15 these two resurrections are referred to as "the resurrection of both the righteous and the wicked."

But the Bible clearly teaches there will be more than two
resurrections. There will be a resurrection of Church Age saints
at the time of the Rapture, before the Tribulation begins (1
Thess. 4:13–18). At the end of the Tribulation, Old Testament
saints and Tribulation martyrs will be resurrected (Dan. 12:1–
2 and Rev. 20:4). And finally, all the unjust who have ever
lived and died outside a faith relationship with God will be
resurrected at the end of the Millennium (Rev. 20:11–12).

Once again, these seemingly conflicting passages present
a problem of reconciliation. How can the promise of two resurrections be reconciled with the depiction of three?

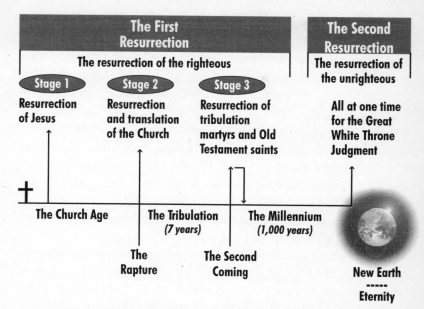

Figure 8: The End-time Sequence of Resurrections

Actually, the solution is rather simple. It seems clear that when the Bible speaks of two resurrections, it is speaking of two in kind, not two in number. The resurrection of the unjust will occur all at one time. The resurrection of the just will occur in stages, and the stages will correspond with the three stages of a Jewish harvest: the first fruits, followed by the general harvest, and concluded with the gleanings. Jesus was the "first fruits" (1 Cor. 15:23). The general harvest will occur at the Rapture when the Church Age saints will be resurrected and the living saints will be translated. The gleanings will occur at the end of the Tribulation at the second coming of Jesus. That is when the Old Testament saints and Tribulation martyrs will be resurrected.

Why will Russia invade Israel in the end times?

Ezekiel 38:4 says the Lord will "put hooks" into the jaws of a Russian coalition and will compel them to come against Israel "in the latter years" (Ezek. 38:8). Later in the chapter it states that the hook will be the desire "to capture spoil and to seize plunder" (Ezek. 38:12).

Prophecy teachers have long argued that the prize that will lure the Russians will most likely be the mineral riches of the Dead Sea, or perhaps a major oil strike in Israel. Tim LaHaye and Jerry Jenkins in their "Left Behind" series devise a very clever and imaginative alternative — the development by an Israeli scientist of a high-powered fertilizer that converts the desert into fertile farmland.[8] This "miracle formula" quickly transforms Israel into one of the richest nations on earth.

This novel concept is not without biblical basis. There are several passages, like Isaiah 35:1, which prophesy that the wilderness and desert will blossom in the end times. But the context of these passages seems to place this phenomenon within the millennial reign of Jesus, when the curse will be partially lifted, and the earth will be refreshed.

I believe the prize the Russians will come after will be the Arab oil fields of the Middle East, and I believe the Russian invasion of Israel will play a far more important part in end-time events than the "Left Behind" series portrays. Here's what I think is the most likely scenario:

- The Palestinian Authority will try to take Jerusalem.

- The Israelis will destroy the Palestinian forces quickly.

- The Palestinians will call for the Arab nations to come to their rescue.

- The Arab nations surrounding Israel will launch an all-out missile attack on Haifa and Tel Aviv.

- The Israelis will resort to nuclear weapons, completely destroying the city of Damascus (Jer. 49 and Isa. 17).

- The Arab world will then call for its natural ally, Russia, to come to its aid.

- The Russians will gleefully respond to this invitation by launching an invasion of Israel. Ostensibly, the

Russians will come to destroy Israel, but their ultimate goal will be to take the Arab oil fields.

- The Russians will be supernaturally destroyed in Israel.

- The whole world will be thrown into a panic.

- A dynamic, charismatic leader will suddenly arise in the European Community who will seem to have the perfect plan to bring peace to the Middle East.

In summary, I see the Russian invasion as ushering in both the rise of the Antichrist and the events leading up to a Middle East peace treaty that will mark the start of the Tribulation.

Where is the United States in the Book of Revelation?

Many have argued that the great international power described in Revelation 18 as dominating the world's economy is the United States. That argument is understandable, particularly since the collapse of the Soviet Union left the United States as the dominant world power. But that interpretation is completely out of line with the context of Revelation 18. The context makes it clear that the chapter is speaking of the world empire of the Antichrist.

So, where is the United States in Revelation? How could the world's only superpower be ignored? Amusingly, some commentators, in their desperation to find the United States, have argued that America is referred to symbolically in Revelation 12:14 where the text says that the Jews will flee Israel in the middle of the Tribulation on "the two wings of the great eagle." The reasoning is that the eagle is the national symbol of the United States, and therefore this passage indicates that the United States will provide an end-time airlift for the Jewish remnant that decides to flee from the Antichrist.

People who interpret the Bible in such bizarre and silly ways forget that the Bible is its own best interpreter. A quick check of the word "eagle" in any concordance will reveal that the term is used in the very same way with regard to the Jew's deliverance from Egyptian captivity. Exodus 19:4 says that they

fled Egypt "on eagles' wings." This is obviously symbolic language indicating that they fled under the protection of Almighty God. Here's how it is put in Deuteronomy 32:11 —
"Like an eagle that stirs up its nest . . . He [the Lord] spread
His wings and caught them, He carried them on His pinions."

So, where then is the United States in Revelation? The
answer is that America is not there. And this fact, in turn,
simply spawns another question: "Why not?" The answer is
that no one knows for sure.

There are several possible explanations for the absence
of the United States in Bible prophecy. Perhaps America will
suffer an economic collapse from which it will never recover
— a collapse so severe that the nation will be reduced to a
Third World status, as happened to Russia when the Soviet
government fell. Or, perhaps the United States will be destroyed by a pre-emptive nuclear attack when Russia invades
Israel. But most likely, the Rapture is the event that will dev-
astate America. I say that because no other nation has so many
born-again Christians in positions of power — both politically and economically. In short, the Rapture will throw the
United States into chaos.

Are the judgments during the Tribulation sequential in nature?

Scholars who reject the premillennial interpretation of
end-time prophecy have always played games with the Book
of Revelation in order to get around the clear teaching in chapter 20 that Jesus is going to return and reign for a thousand
years.

Some have spiritualized this passage into nothingness.
Others have argued that the judgments in Revelation are repetitive rather than sequential. Their argument is that the seal,
trumpet, and bowl judgments are all descriptions of the same
thing — namely, the destruction of Jerusalem that occurred
about 40 years after the establishment of the Church. So, in
Revelation 19, Jesus is seen as returning in A.D. 70 to pour
out God's wrath on the Jews, and chapter 20 is viewed as His

subsequent reign over the Church. There are certainly flash-backs and flash-forwards in the Book of Revelation, but most of the action is clearly sequential in nature, and that is the biblical approach that is incorporated into the "Left Behind" series.[9]

The judgments are definitely not circular or repetitive in nature. The seal judgments kill one-fourth of humanity (Rev. 6:8). The trumpet judgments result in the death of one-third of those remaining (Rev. 9:15). The bowl judgments do not result in massive deaths at all. Instead, they produce wide-spread intense suffering, and the fifth bowl (darkness) is focused upon the capital of the Antichrist (Rev. 16:1–16).

To argue that Revelation 20 portrays Jesus' reign over the world through the Church, one would have to spiritualize the thousand years, since the Church has existed almost 2,000 years. The chapter refers six times to the reign of Jesus lasting a thousand years. What would God have to say to convince us that He means a thousand years?

Also, it is painfully clear that the Church is not reigning over the world. Jesus may be reigning over His church, but He obviously is not reigning over the world through His church, for all the nations of the earth are in rebellion against God and His Anointed One (Ps. 2).

Is the portrayal of the Antichrist in the "Left Behind" series biblically accurate?

The portrayal of the Antichrist in the "Left Behind" series is solidly biblical. He is pictured as arising out of Romania,[10] and this is in accordance with the Bible's concept that he will come from an area that was included in the old Roman Empire and that he will be of Roman heritage (Dan. 9:26).

He is described as handsome and brilliant and initially self-effacing and humble.[11] As he garners power, he begins to display flashes of egomania,[12] and he begins to display super-natural powers such as mass hypnosis and mind reading.[13] He ultimately deteriorates into a totally self-possessed person who begins to believe that he is God.[14] All of this is in accordance

with the descriptions contained in Daniel's prophecies (Dan.
8:23–26 and 11:36–38).

The place where I believe the "Left Behind" series gets off
base regarding the Antichrist is when the story line portrays
him raising his right-hand man from the dead.[15] No such event
is recorded in the Scriptures. Furthermore, the Bible says that
Jesus now has the keys to death (Rev. 1:18), and I do not believe He is ever going to share that power with anyone, particularly the Antichrist or Satan. The Antichrist will have supernatural powers given to him by Satan (Dan. 8:24), but I do not
believe they will include the power to raise people from the dead.

Will the Antichrist be killed and resurrected from the dead?

The authors of the "Left Behind" series assert that the
Antichrist will be assassinated[16] and then be resurrected from
the dead.[17] There is a biblical basis for this assumption, but I
do not believe it is valid. The assumption is based on Revelation 13:1–3 where John says he saw "a beast coming up out of
the sea" (the Antichrist rising from among the Gentile nations). He then adds that the beast had ten horns with crowns
and seven heads, and that one of his heads "had been slain,"
and "the fatal wound had been healed."

This is obviously symbolic imagery, and I believe it refers to kingdoms rather than a person. In Revelation 12:3 Satan
is portrayed as a dragon with seven crowned heads and ten
horns. In Revelation 13:1 the Antichrist is pictured as a beast
with seven heads and ten crowned horns. Satan's heads are
crowned because they represent the seven great world empires
which he has controlled. The Antichrist's ten horns are
crowned because they represent the ten kingdoms he will initially control.

A clue to the identity of the seven heads is located in
Revelation 17:9–11 where the imagery of seven mountains is
used to refer to the great kingdoms of the world. We are told
that at the time John was writing (about A.D. 95), "five had
fallen, one is, the other has not yet come" (Rev. 17:10). That
would mean that the kingdoms past, in order, would be Egypt,

Assyria, Babylon, Medo-Persia, and Greece. The current kingdom ("one is") was Rome. The one yet to come is the kingdom of the Antichrist which will be based initially on control of ten kingdoms, but will expand into a worldwide empire which will be the eighth and last of the Gentile world kingdoms (Rev. 17:11).

So, I believe the "head" referred to in Revelation 13:3 which is slain and then resurrected is the Roman Empire, and not an individual. We are witnessing that resurrection today in the emergence of the European Union.

Where will the Antichrist's headquarters be located?

LaHaye and Jenkins portray the Antichrist moving the headquarters of the United Nations from New York to Babylon[18] and changing the name of the organization to the Global Community.[19]

There is a strong biblical basis for believing that Babylon will be the capital of the Antichrist's world empire. Revelation 17 pictures Babylon as the headquarters of the Antichrist, and Revelation 18 describes the destruction of the city by God and equates it with the destruction of the Antichrist's world kingdom.

But there is a problem with these passages. Revelation 17 actually states that the capital will be "mystery Babylon" (verse 5), which I believe is a clear indication that the author is speaking symbolically. Later in the chapter, two clues are given as to the identity of the city. First, it is described as the city of "seven mountains" (verse 9). Second, it is described as "the great city which reigns over the kings of the earth" (verse 18). I believe these descriptions make it clear that "mystery Babylon" is Rome. John could not name Rome because he was a Roman prisoner, so he described the city symbolically and then gave us clues that could only point to Rome.

Furthermore, Isaiah 13:17–20 says that when Babylon is destroyed by the Medes, it will "never be inhabited or lived in from generation to generation." There are some, like Charles Dyer, who have tried to argue that Babylon is being rebuilt today.[20] But the only rebuilding has been for tourist purposes, not for large-scale habitation.

So, I believe the capital of the Antichrist's empire, both politically and spiritually, will be the city of Rome.

Why was the number 666 used as a symbol of the Antichrist?

There are three good reasons this number was used. The first is the fact that in the Scriptures, the number of man is 6 because man was created on the sixth day. In contrast, the number of God is 7 because it represents completion and perfection, since on the seventh day of creation, God rested from His work which He declared to be good or perfect.

Now, in the Hebrew language, superlatives are expressed by repeating the word or phrase, the ultimate being its repetition three times. Thus, when Isaiah saw the Lord lifted up and exalted in the Temple, he heard Seraphim singing, "Holy, holy, holy is the Lord of hosts" (Isa. 6:1–3). The number 666 therefore represents the number of man carried to its zenith.

The use of this number is most appropriate because during the Tribulation, Satan will work to exalt his man, the Antichrist, as the world's Messiah. Furthermore, on the earth at that time there will be a demonic trinity who will represent the humanistic aspirations of man — Satan, masquerading as God; the Antichrist, pretending to be the Messiah; and the false prophet, mimicking the role of the Holy Spirit by pointing people to the false messiah.

The second reason the number 666 is used is because of its symbolism in Jewish thinking. The Bible tells us that in the year in which King Solomon received 666 talents of gold, he turned his back on God and became obsessed with women, horses, and money (1 Kings 10:14 and 2 Chron. 9:13). Thus, in Jewish history, the number 666 came to stand for apostasy.

The third reason the number is used is related to the fact that in both Hebrew and Greek, the letters of the alphabet also stand for numbers. This makes it possible to add up a numerical value for every name. The Antichrist's name will add up to 666 in either Greek or Hebrew (or perhaps both) and will thus be an expression of the ultimate apostasy — presenting one's self as a substitute for the real Messiah.

Who are the two witnesses who will preach in Jerusalem?

Revelation 11 says there will be two miracle-working witnesses of God who will preach in Jerusalem for three and one-half years. They will serve as the conscience of the world and will be hated by most people. The Antichrist will kill them at the mid-point of the Tribulation, and the world will rejoice.

The mystery regarding these witnesses has always been their identity. Who will they be? The Book of Revelation does not tell us. LaHaye postulates that they will be Moses and Elijah,[21] and there is good biblical evidence for this conclusion. These two were present at Jesus' transfiguration (Matt. 17:3). Also, the miracles performed by the two witnesses (described in Rev. 11:6) are those that characterized the ministries of Moses and Elijah.

Still, I believe the two most likely candidates are Enoch and Elijah. Both were men of righteousness who were raptured to heaven. Neither experienced death. Both were prophets, and one was a Gentile (Enoch) and the other was a Jew (Elijah).

I think it is interesting that this was the unanimous opinion of the Church Fathers during the first three hundred years of the Church. All of them identified the two witnesses in their writings as Enoch and Elijah.[22] One, by the name of Haymo, who served as the bishop of Halberstadt (840–853), even quotes a version of Malachi 4:5 as stating that both Enoch and Elijah will appear before the Day of the Lord.[23] Our modern versions mention only Elijah.

So, we know for certain from the passage in Malachi that one of the two witnesses will be Elijah. The identity of the other is unknown. He could be either Moses or Enoch. I side with Enoch because he was a Gentile, and I believe the Lord is going to supply two witnesses instead of one because He is

going to ordain one to speak to the Jews and the other to the
Gentiles.

Will all believers during the Tribulation be marked on the forehead?

The most surprising thing I have thus far encountered in
the "Left Behind" series is the idea that about two years into
the Tribulation, those who have placed their faith in Jesus will
receive a supernatural identifying mark on their foreheads that
can only be seen by fellow believers.[24]

The authors indicate that they base this idea upon a statement in Revelation 7:3 which says that a special group of
144,000 people will be "sealed as the bond-servants of God
on their foreheads." But the context of that verse makes it
crystal clear that this sealing applies only to 144,000 Jews who
will accept Jesus as their Messiah and who will be ordained
by God to serve Him during the Tribulation. There is never
any indication in this passage of this mark being applied to
anyone else.

Perhaps LaHaye draws his inference that all believers will
be sealed from Revelation 9 which describes a plague of demonic locusts which will be let loose to torment unbelievers.
In Revelation 9:4 it states that the locusts are told they cannot
harm those who "have the seal of God on their foreheads." I
have always assumed this was a reference back to the 144,000
Jews, but it could, of course, refer to all believers, and I hope
that is the meaning.

What did Jesus mean when He said, "I have the keys of death and hades"?

To grasp the meaning of this statement made in Revelation 1:18, you must first of all understand some things the Bible
teaches about death. The Scriptures define death as the separa-
tion of the spirit from the body (2 Cor. 5:8 and James 2:26).
The body goes into the grave, and before the Cross, all spirits
of the dead went to a place called hades (*sheol* in the Old Testament). Hades contained two compartments, one for the saved,
which Jesus called "Abraham's bosom," and one for the lost,

which he called "torments" (Luke 16:14–31). "Abraham's bosom" was also known in Jewish thought as "paradise" (Luke 23:43). The two compartments were separated by an abyss that no one could cross.

When Jesus died on the cross, He descended into hades to make the glorious proclamation that He had shed His blood for the remission of sins (1 Pet. 3:18–20). When He later ascended to heaven, He took with Him all the saved people who had been confined to hades (Eph. 4:8). In other words, when Jesus ascended, He moved paradise from hades to heaven. Paul confirmed this in 2 Corinthians 12 where he states he was caught up to heaven, which he then identifies as paradise (2 Cor. 12:1–4).

The Biblical Concept of Hades

Why did all this change at the Cross? Why is it that before the Cross the spirits of the saved went to hades, and since the Cross they go directly to heaven? The answer is that Old Testament saints could not go directly to heaven because their salvation was not complete. Their sins had been covered by

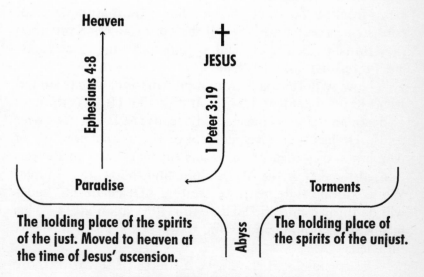

Figure 9: The Biblical Concept of Hades

their faith, but not forgiven, for there can be no forgiveness of sins apart from the shedding of blood (Lev. 17:11 and Heb. 9:22). When the Messiah's blood was shed, the sins of Old Testament saints were forgiven, and they could enter the presence of their Holy God.

So, to summarize, since the time of the Cross, the spirits of all believers go directly to heaven at death whereas the spirits of the lost still go to hades to that terrible holding place called torments.

One very important fact to keep in mind is that hades is not hell. As I said, hades today is a temporary holding place for the spirits of the unjust who have died outside a faith relationship with God. Hell is the ultimate destiny of the unjust. No one is in hell now. The first to be consigned to hell will be the Antichrist and his false prophet (Rev. 19:20). Satan will be committed to "the lake of fire," which is hell, at the end of the Millennium (Rev. 20:10). Satan is not in charge of hell, as medieval poets and writers pictured. He will be tormented there, together with the Antichrist, the false prophet and all those who are lost.

The confusion about the difference in hades and hell stems from the fact that the King James translators were not consistent in their translation of the word "hades." Sometimes they transliterated it as "hades," but sometimes they translated it (erroneously) as "hell."

Now, with this background information, we can understand Jesus' statement. His declaration that He has "the keys of death and Hades" means that because of His victory over death, He has been given control of the ultimate destiny of people's bodies (death) and souls (hades). Later in Revelation, at the end of the Millennium, and following the Great White Throne Judgment, we are told that death and hades will be thrown into the lake of fire (Revelation 20:14). This means that both the bodies and spirits of the lost will be cast into hell.

Jesus' statement should be a source of terror to those who have rejected Him as Lord and Savior. But for those who have put their hope and trust in Him, it should be a source of great joy and peace, for Jesus is assuring John that those who put their faith in Him will overcome death, just as He did. This glorious declaration is a reminder of what Jesus said to Martha in front of the tomb of Lazarus: "I am the resurrection and the life; he who believes in Me shall live even if he dies" (John 11:25).

Will we know each other in heaven?

I don't think I have ever conducted a prophecy conference where this question was not asked. In responding, let me first of all remind you that the Bible never says we will live eternally in heaven. The Bible teaches instead that the redeemed will live eternally on a new, perfected earth. Further, the Scriptures state that God will come to earth and live in our presence in the New Jerusalem (Rev. 21:1–7). Since heaven is wherever God resides, this means that heaven will come to earth. So, in that sense, and that sense only, the redeemed will reside in heaven forever.

And yes, we will certainly know each other. We are told that we will have glorified bodies like the one that Jesus had after His resurrection (Phil. 3:21). Once the disciples got over the shock of Jesus' resurrection, they easily recognized Him whenever He appeared to them (John 21:1–7). In like manner, the disciples recognized Moses and Elijah when they appeared at the transfiguration of Jesus (Matt. 17:1–5).

We do not become non-entities at death. We retain our individuality and personality. God constantly refers to himself in the Scriptures as "the God of Abraham, Isaac, and Jacob" long after their deaths. His fellowship with them is obviously continuing in heaven. Paul confirmed recognition after death in his writings when he told the people he had converted in Thessalonica that they would be his "hope or joy or crown of righteousness" when they stood "in the presence of the Lord Jesus Christ at His coming" (1 Thess. 2:19). Paul was looking forward to being with them and enjoying their fellowship in heaven.

What did Jesus mean when He stated that He will bring rewards when He returns? And what did He mean when He said those rewards would be related to what we have done? Doesn't this teach salvation by good works as opposed to salvation by grace through faith?

The statement in this question is found in Revelation 22:12 — "Behold, I am coming quickly, and My reward is with Me, to render to every man according to what he has done."

Again, we have a problem of reconciliation, because the Bible clearly and emphatically teaches that salvation comes by grace through faith and not by works (Eph. 2:8–10 and Titus 3:5). But again, this is a "problem" that is easily solved.

It is true that our eternal destiny — whether heaven or hell — is determined in this life by whether or not we accept Jesus as Lord and Savior (1 John 5:5). It is also true that this salvation is a gift of God received by faith, and not a reward that anyone can earn through good works (Rom. 6:23).

When believers stand before the Lord to be judged (2 Cor. 5:10), they will not be judged of their sins to determine their eternal destiny. That's because their sins have already been judged. They were put upon Jesus as He hung upon the cross. In 2 Corinthians 5:21 it says that God "made Him who knew no sin to be sin on our behalf, that we might become the righteousness of God in Him." Jesus received the wrath of God for our sins, and we who have put our faith in Jesus have had our sins forgiven and forgotten as far as they relate to our eternal destiny (Heb. 8:12).

But we who are believers are going to be judged. We are going to be judged of our works, not to determine our eternal destiny, but to determine our degrees of reward. Here is the way Paul put it in 2 Corinthians 5:10: "For we must all appear before the judgment seat of Christ, that each one may be recompensed for his deeds in the body, according to what he has done, whether good or bad."

The works we have done to advance the Lord's kingdom on this earth are going to be evaluated as to quantity (2 Cor. 5:10), quality (1 Cor. 3:13), and motive (1 Cor. 4:5). When we are born again, the Holy Spirit gifts us (1 Cor. 12:4-7), and we are expected to use those gifts to advance the Lord's kingdom. That's one of the reasons it is so important to be familiar with the spiritual gifts and to be aware of the ones we have been given.

Some of the rewards that the Lord Jesus will give are spelled out in Scripture:

- A crown of righteousness — for those who live their lives with the love of the Lord's appearing in their hearts (2 Tim. 4:7–8).

- A crown of life — for those who persevere under trial (Rev. 2:10 and James 1:12).

- An imperishable wreath — for those who exercise self-control (1 Cor. 9:25).

- A crown of glory — for faithful elders and pastors (1 Pet. 5:4).

- A crown of rejoicing — for soul winners (Phil. 4:1 and 1 Thess. 2:19).

- Robes of fine linen — which will, in some way, reflect the righteous deeds of the saints (Rev. 19:8).

We are told in 1 Corinthians 3:10–15 that some of the redeemed will not receive any special rewards at all. Their worthless works will be "burned up," and they will "suffer loss," for they will not have any reward to place at the feet of Jesus to honor Him — as the 24 elders in heaven are pictured doing before the throne of God (Rev. 4:10).

To summarize, the redeemed do not work to be saved; they work because they are saved. Paul states that we are saved "not on the basis of deeds which we have done in righteousness," but we are saved "to engage in good deeds" (Titus 3:8). The writer of Hebrews puts it this way: "And do not neglect doing good and sharing; for with such sacrifices God is pleased" (Heb. 13:16).

What do you consider to be the fundamental lessons of Revelation?

There are many, for the book is a spiritual gem, full of deep insights about man and God. Let's take a look at some of the most important ones in the next chapter.

Chapter 5

Applying Revelation

Bible prophecy is pie-in-the-sky. It has no earthly practicality. It is a waste of time." I could not begin to tell you how many times I have heard such statements, often from the mouths of pastors. The concept that prophecy is irrelevant to Christian living is widespread and is one of several reasons that prophecy is so terribly ignored in the preaching and teaching programs of most churches.

I don't think I can emphasize too strongly that this idea that Bible prophecy is irrelevant to Christian growth and living is totally unbiblical. The view is really a reflection upon the person who holds it, because it manifests a gross lack of knowledge of God's prophetic word.

The Apostle's Opinions

The New Testament writers speak over and over of the relevance of prophecy to Christian living. Paul resorts to prophecy to call Christians to holiness (Rom. 13:12–14):

The night is almost gone, and the day is at hand.
Let us therefore lay aside the deeds of darkness and
put on the armor of light. Let us behave properly as

in the day, not in carousing and drunkenness, not in
sexual promiscuity and sensuality, not in strife and
jealousy. But put on the Lord Jesus Christ, and make
no provision for the flesh in regard to its lust.

In this passage, Paul reminds his readers that the Lord
can return at any moment and that they should therefore live
holy lives to be prepared for His return. He uses the same
approach in his first letter to Timothy. He urges the young
preacher to "pursue righteousness, godliness, faith, love, perseverance and gentleness" and to "fight the good fight of faith,"
keeping himself free of "stain or reproach until the appearing
of our Lord Jesus Christ" (1 Tim. 6:11–14).

Likewise, in his letter to Titus, Paul relates holy living to
prophecy. He exhorts his readers to live "looking for the blessed
hope and the appearing of the glory of our great God and
Savior, Christ Jesus" (Titus 2:13). He then tells them that as
they live with anticipation of the Lord's imminent return, they
are "to deny ungodliness and worldly desires and to live sensibly, righteously and godly in the present age" (Titus 2:12).

Peter also resorted to prophecy to motivate holy living.
In his first letter to the persecuted and dispersed Christians
of his day and time, he called them to holiness by writing,
"Prepare your minds for action, keep sober in spirit, fix your
hope completely on the grace to be brought to you at the
revelation of Jesus Christ" (1 Pet. 1:13). Then, with the
thought of the Lord's return in their minds, he added, "Like
the Holy One who called you, be holy yourselves also in all
your behavior" (1 Pet. 1:15). In similar manner, Peter reminds
us in his second letter that "entrance into the eternal kingdom of our Lord and Savior Jesus Christ will be abundantly
supplied" to those who are characterized by diligence, moral
excellence, knowledge, self-control, perseverance, godliness,
brotherly kindness and love (2 Pet. 1:5–11). Later in the same
letter, Peter wrote about the future destruction of the earth
by fire after the Lord returns (2 Pet. 3:7–10). He then ob-
served, "Since all these things are to be destroyed in this way,

what sort of people ought you to be in holy conduct and god-liness" (2 Pet. 3:11).

The apostle John joined the chorus of voices emphasiz-ing the relationship of Bible prophecy to holiness. He wrote that everyone who lives with their hope fixed on Jesus' return "purifies himself, just as He is pure" (1 John 3:1–3).

Two Transforming Truths

In my 20 years of preaching and teaching Bible proph-ecy, I have experienced the truth of these statements. I have discovered that if you convince Christians of two truths re-lated to Bible prophecy, their lives will be transformed because they will be motivated to commit their lives to holiness and evangelism.

What are those two truths? The first is that Jesus really is going to return. I have found that most Christians believe this truth in their minds, but not in their hearts. And that is a shame, because a belief will not begin to affect the way we think and behave until it moves from the mind to the heart.

The second, related truth is that Jesus can return at any moment. This crucial truth is not even held mentally by most professing Christians. To the average Christian, the timing of the Lord's return is something relegated to the distant future. There is no sense of imminence.

Again, when any person begins to believe that Jesus re-ally is coming back and that His return can occur any mo-ment, that person will be motivated to live a holy life and share the gospel with others. That, in part, is the relevance of Bible prophecy to how we live here and now.

Building Hope

I say "in part," because Bible prophecy is relevant to our current lives in another way. It relates to the strength of the hope that we live with. Our God is a "God of hope" (Rom. 15:13), and He expresses that hope to us in the promises He makes about the future. Those promises give us hope as we struggle with the challenges of life here and now.

The promises are beyond anything we could ever imagine. Paul put it this way: "The sufferings of this present time are not worthy to be compared with the glory that is to be revealed to us" (Rom. 8:18). That is an incredible statement. All of us know people who are suffering mightily from physical ailments like cancer and from emotional afflictions like depression. But Paul says no matter what we may suffer, that suffering is *nothing* compared to the glories God has prepared for those who love Him. In 1 Corinthians 2:9 Paul expresses a similar sentiment. He says that no eye has seen and no ear has heard, nor has the mind of man conceived what God has prepared for those who love Him. But in the very next verse, he says those things have been revealed to us through the Holy Spirit (1 Cor. 2:10). And how has the Spirit revealed them? Through the prophecies in God's Word.

Prophecy has often been a playground for fanatics. But it can also be green pastures for those who approach it sensibly and responsibly, seeking to know Jesus more intimately and to better understand God's will for their lives. The Book of Revelation is no exception. So, let's search its pages for some spiritual insights that will aid us spiritually in our Christian growth and our fight to overcome the world.

Our Creator Is a God of Prophecy

Revelation 19:10 says that "the testimony of Jesus is the spirit of prophecy." Revelation 22:6 refers to the Lord as "the God of the spirits of the prophets." These statements need to be considered carefully by those who hold prophecy in contempt.

One of the unique characteristics of our God is that He knows the future. Read what He says about himself in Isaiah 46:9–11:

> For I am God, and there is no other;
> I am God, and there is no one like Me,
> Declaring the end from the beginning
> And from ancient times things which have not
>   been done,
> Saying, "My purpose will be established,

And I will accomplish all My good pleasure. . . ."
Truly I have spoken; truly I will bring it to pass.
I have planned it, surely I will do it.

This is a remarkable passage. God declares that He is the one and only true God and that proof of this is to be found in the fact that He knows what is going to happen in the future. Not only does He know the future, but He proclaims it through prophetic utterances. Finally, He says that His boldness in declaring the future is rooted in His power to accomplish whatever He wills.

This is the reason that Daniel could state with confidence that "there is a God in heaven who reveals mysteries" of "what will take place in the latter days" (Dan. 2:28). Echoing this sentiment, the prophet Amos wrote, "Surely the Lord God does nothing unless He reveals His secret counsel to His servants the prophets" (Amos 3:7).

That does not mean that God has revealed everything He plans to do in the future. But what He has revealed is enough to give us great hope. He has promised that when Jesus returns, the living and dead in Christ will both be caught up to meet Him in the sky. They will be glorified (receive immortal bodies), and when the Tribulation is finished, they will return to earth to reign with Jesus over a world flooded with peace, righteousness, and justice. Further, He has promised that after Jesus' millennial reign, the redeemed will live eternally with both the Father and the Son inside a New Jerusalem located on a new, perfected earth.

I have had people tell me that they do not believe God wants us to know anything about the future because "we are called to live by faith and not by sight." That is nonsense. Knowing the promises of God about the future does not mean we cease to walk by faith. The promises must be believed if they are to be meaningful, and that requires faith.

But for prophecy to have an impact on our lives, we must believe it came from God, that it means what it says, and that it will one day be fulfilled. Peter assured us that Bible prophecy is from God when He declared that the Hebrew prophets were guided in their prophecies by "the Spirit of Christ within them" (1 Pet. 1:11). That's an interesting statement. Think about it for a moment. The Spirit of Christ operated within the prophets to point them to the Christ!

That Bible prophecy means what it says can be deduced from the fact that the First Coming prophecies were all literally fulfilled. Take the prophecies of Zechariah for example. He prophesied that the Messiah would come humbly on a donkey, be hailed as a king, and be betrayed for 30 pieces of silver (Zech. 9:9 and 11:12). He also said the Messiah would be lifted up and pierced (Zech. 13:6). All of these prophecies were fulfilled in their plain sense meaning in the life of Jesus. Should we not, therefore, expect Zechariah's Second Coming prophecies to be literally fulfilled?

Consider Psalm 22, a psalm written 1,000 years before the birth of Jesus. The first two-thirds of it pertain to the crucifixion of the Messiah. We are told that He will be despised and publicly sneered at (Ps. 22:6–7). He will be attacked by demons as He hangs on His execution stake (Ps. 22:12–13), and He will suffer terrible physical torment (Ps. 22:14–15). The psalm says further that He will have His hands and feet pierced (Ps. 22:16) and that His executioners will cast lots for His garments (Ps. 22:18). Matthew records the literal fulfillment of every one of these prophecies (Matt. 26 and 27).

The last third of Psalm 22 contains prophecies about the end times. We are told that "all the ends of the earth will remember and turn to the Lord" and "all the families of the nations will worship" before Him (Ps. 22:27). The passage further states that the Messiah will "rule over the nations" (Ps. 22:28). Shouldn't we expect these end-time prophecies to be literally fulfilled, just as the First Coming prophecies were? If not, why not?

The Book of Revelation declares itself to be prophecy (Rev. 1:3 and 22:7). As such, it is not some Alice in Wonderland fantasy story for adults. It outlines actual events that are going to occur in the future. There is going to be 7 years of unparalleled tribulation followed by 1,000 years of glorious righteousness which, in turn, will be followed by eternity on a new earth. You can scoff at it or believe it. But regardless of what you do, God is going to fulfill what He has promised because He is faithful.

That's why there is a rainbow around His throne (Rev. 4:3). It is there to symbolize that He is a God who keeps His promises, just as He has honored His promise to never destroy the earth again by water (Gen. 9:11). That's also the reason He is called "the Faithful and True" One (Rev. 19:11).

Our Creator Is a Personal, Caring God

The first three chapters of Revelation are a tremendous testimony to this truth. And what a glorious truth it is!

Christianity's concept of a personal, caring God is unique. With the exception of Christianity and biblical Judaism, the rest of the world's religions postulate a god who is aloof, distant, uncaring, and uninvolved with the creation except for occasional, impulsive interventions. Modern-day rabbinical Judaism (which was developed after the destruction of the temple in A.D. 70) does not have a personal god. Instead, He is a god who relates to the Jews corporately as a nation.

In sharp contrast to the aloof and uncaring god of the world's pagan religions, the Bible reveals a God who is personal and caring, and who is intimately involved with His creation. That, in fact, is the fundamental message of the first three chapters of Revelation. Jesus returns to the island of Patmos 65 years after His death, burial, and resurrection to assure a persecuted Church that He knows about their suffering, that He cares, and that He will see them through to victory.

Although I was born into a Christian family and raised in the Church, it took me 30 years to discover the personal nature of my God. That's because I was taught that the God of the Bible retired in the first century, becoming the "Grand Old Man in the Sky." With His retirement, the miraculous ceased, and we were left to cope with life with our minds, talents, and the wisdom of His Word. I had no knowledge of the realm of the supernatural, including demons, angels, and spiritual warfare. I was a sitting duck for spiritual attack and defeat.

Through a serious of wilderness experiences, I was brought to the end of myself and driven into God's Word. That's when I made what was, for me, an amazing discovery. My eyes were opened to the undeniable fact that God has not changed — that the personal, loving, caring God of the Bible is still the God of today.

In Malachi 3:6 God declares, "I, the Lord, do not change." In the New Testament, Jesus refers to God as "the Father of lights, with whom there is no variation, or shifting shadow" (James 1:17). The clincher is found in Hebrews 13:8 — "Jesus Christ is the same yesterday and today, yes and forever."

What could be clearer? God is still on the throne. He still hears prayers. He still performs miracles. He is just as concerned about every person on earth today as He was in Old Testament times or when His Son walked this earth in New Testament times.

The irony is that we can limit His impact in our lives by our lack of faith, just as the people of Nazareth limited the power of Jesus by their unbelief (Mark 6:1–6). We can put God in a box, as I did for 30 years, by denying that He can still operate today as He did in Bible times.

My own turnaround came when I was in desperate need and stumbled across a verse in Peter's first epistle that jumped off the page, grabbed me by the throat, and shook me until my teeth rattled! It said, "Humble yourselves, therefore, under the mighty hand of God, that He may exalt you at the proper time, casting all your anxiety on Him, because He cares for you" (1 Pet. 5:6–7). The words, "HE CARES FOR YOU," hit me like a bomb!

Once I started believing in a personal God who is concerned about all my needs and struggles, I began to discover verses all through the Bible which confirmed my newfound discovery:

Just as a father has compassion on his children, so the Lord has compassion on those who fear Him (Ps. 103:13).

Who is like the Lord our God, Who is enthroned on high, Who humbles Himself to behold The things that are in heaven and in the earth? He raises the poor from the dust And lifts the needy from the ash heap (Ps. 113:5–7).

For the devious are an abomination to the Lord; but He is intimate with the upright (Prov. 3:32).

The Lord longs to be gracious to you, And therefore He waits on high to have compassion on you. For the Lord is a God of justice (Isa. 30:18).

The Lord is good, A stronghold in the day of trouble, And He knows those who take refuge in Him (Nah. 1:7).

Are not five sparrows sold for two cents? And yet not one of them is forgotten before God. Indeed, the very hairs of your head are numbered. Do not fear; you are of more value than many sparrows (Mat. 12:6–7).

Be anxious about nothing, but in everything by prayer and supplication with thanksgiving let your requests be made known to God. And the peace of God, which surpasses all comprehension, shall guard your hearts and your minds in Christ Jesus (Phil. 4:6–7).

And my God shall supply all your needs according to His riches in glory in Christ Jesus (Phil. 4:19).

Blessed be the God and Father of our Lord Jesus Christ, the Father of mercies and God of all comfort (1 Cor. 1:3).

Draw near to God and He will draw near to
you (James 4:8).

Perhaps the greatest statement of God's loving concern
for us is contained in Jesus' Sermon on the Mount. Jesus reminds us that God cares for the birds of the air and the lilies
of the field. He then asks a rhetorical question: "If God feeds
the birds, won't He care for us? Are we not worth much more
than they?" (Matt. 6:26–27, paraphrased). To emphasize His
point, He then asks a similar question: "If God so clothes the
grass of the field [like King Solomon in his glory], which is
alive today and tomorrow is thrown into the furnace, will He
not much more clothe you?" He then adds a lament, "You of
little faith!" (Matt. 6:30).

God loves His creation. He sacrificed His Son to redeem
it — all of it. He desires fellowship with His creatures, and He
desires that fellowship so much that when the new, eternal
earth is created, He is going to descend to that earth to live
among mankind (Rev. 21:3). He will allow the redeemed to
see His face (Rev. 22:4), and we will serve Him forever (Rev.
22:3). What glorious promises! What a wonderful expectation
we have! What an incredible God! "You, O Lord, are a God
merciful and gracious, slow to anger and abundant in
lovingkindness and truth" (Ps. 86:15).

Our Creator Is Sovereign

The Book of Revelation is a powerful testimony of the
sovereignty of God. In the opening verses God declares, "I
am the Alpha and the Omega who is and who was and who is
to come, the Almighty" (Rev. 1:8). At the end of the book
John records Jesus speaking similar words about himself,
making it clear that He is God in the flesh: "I am the Alpha
and the Omega, the first and the last, the beginning and the
end" (Rev. 22:13).

When John is raptured to the throne room of God at the
beginning of chapter 4, he hears the heavenly host singing
about God's sovereignty: "Holy, Holy, Holy, is the Lord God,

the Almighty, who was and who is and who is to come" (Rev. 4:8). He is holy. He is eternal. He is omnipotent — "the Almighty One." In chapter 5 the songs glorify the Lamb of God, His Son. One of them specifically mentions that the Son has been given "dominion forever and ever" (Rev. 5:13).

The Book of Revelation then proceeds to tell the story of how God will exercise His sovereignty during the Tribulation to subdue both the kings of the earth and the prince of the air — namely, Satan. The result is the return of God's Son to exercise sovereignty over all the world in His reign of a thousand years. We are told that He will rule in absolute sovereignty with "a rod of iron" (Rev. 2:27 and 19:15).

Many claim Jesus is reigning now, but that cannot be, for all the nations in the world are in revolt against God and His Anointed One. To those who insist that Jesus is now reigning over the world, I always respond by saying, "If that is true, then He is doing a very poor job, for all the world is caught up in rebellion against Him."

Jesus is currently serving as our high priest before the throne of His Father, interceding in behalf of the redeemed (Heb. 8:1–2 and 9:11). The writer of Hebrews calls Him "the Apostle and High Priest of our confession" (Heb. 3:1), and he says that in that capacity, He "makes propitiation for the sins of the people" (Heb. 2:17). This is the reason that when Jesus appeared to John on the island of Patmos, He appeared dressed as a high priest, "clothed in a robe reaching to the feet, and girded across His chest with a golden sash" (Rev. 1:13).

When Jesus returns at the end of the Tribulation, He will come as "King of kings and Lord of lords" (Rev. 19:16). He will come to take back the dominion over planet Earth that Satan stole from Adam and Eve when they sinned. Satan will be bound so that he can no longer deceive the nations (Rev. 20:1–3), and Jesus will begin to exercise sovereignty over all the earth (Rev. 20:4–6).

The point that many fail to grasp is that several benefits of the Cross are delayed. It is true that Jesus defeated Satan on the Cross through the power of His resurrection, but all

aspects of that defeat have not yet been realized in history.
The resurrection of the saints has not yet occurred. The redeemed have not yet received their glorified bodies. And Satan has not yet been deprived of his sovereignty over planet
Earth.

With regard to dominion, the writer of Hebrews puts it
this way: "You [the Father] have put all things in subjection
under His [Jesus'] feet, for in subjecting all things to Him
[Jesus], He [the Father] left nothing that is not subject to Him.
But now we do not yet see all things subjected to Him" (Heb.
2:8, emphasis added).

Jesus has earned the sovereignty that man lost in Eden,
but He has not yet claimed it. He is a king in waiting, just as
David was for many years. Samuel anointed David to be king
of all Israel, but David had to wait a long time to claim his
throne. He did not actually become king until God was ready
to bring Saul's reign to an end.

That's why, long after the Cross, John wrote that "the
whole world lies in the power of the evil one" (1 John 5:19). In
other words, Satan is still the "ruler of this world" (John 12:31).
And that's the reason he still "prowls about like a roaring lion,
seeking someone to devour" (1 Pet. 5:8).

But Revelation makes it clear that Satan's days are numbered. The time is fast approaching when Jesus will return,
and Satan will be crushed under the feet of the redeemed (Rom.
16:20). That's when Jesus will proclaim, "The kingdom of the
world has become the kingdom of our Lord, and of His Christ,
and He will reign forever and ever" (Rev. 11:15).

Until that time, Satan will continue to serve as the prince
of this world, but he will operate under the superintending
sovereignty of God. Satan is not omnipotent. He cannot do
anything he pleases. He had to beg God's permission to touch
Job (Job 1:6–12). Satan has deceived himself into believing
that He can outsmart the Lord. He has to be the most frus-
trated person in the universe because no matter what he does,
God takes it and uses it to accomplish His purposes.

Take the crucifixion for example. Satan thought he had

his greatest victory when he motivated mankind to nail the Son of God to a cross. But God took that dastardly event and converted it into a glorious one through the power of the resurrection.

Likewise, Satan certainly must have thought he had engineered a great victory when he manipulated the nations of the world to slaughter each other on the battlefields of World War I. But God worked through the horror of that war to liberate Palestine from the Turks and prepare it as a homeland for the Jews. Satan must have panicked over that development, because his next move was to motivate the launching of a holocaust that was designed to annihilate the Jewish people. But out of the ashes of World War II came a Jewish people who were determined to return to their homeland and establish their own state. God worked through Satan's evil in World War I to prepare the land of Israel for the Jewish people. He worked through Satan's evil in World War II to prepare the Jewish people for their homeland. It is no wonder that the Scriptures say that God sits in heaven and laughs at the attempts of Satan and mankind to frustrate His will in history (Ps. 2:1–4).

Our Creator Is Serious about Sin

I believe most people, including many Christians, view God as a great cosmic teddy bear. To them, He is soft and cuddly and easy to deceive. He is a God of infinite love who would "never hurt a fly."

This sentimental, syrupy view of God is shattered by the Book of Revelation. The Lord is revealed as a Holy God who will not tolerate unrepentant sin.

The book begins with Jesus rebuking His churches for their sins (chapters 2 and 3). He chastises them for their legalism, liberalism, pagan and cultic practices, deadness, worldliness, and apathy. At times He speaks to them with startling fierceness, as when He calls the church at Thyatira to stop tolerating a self-proclaimed prophetess who was luring them into immorality and idolatry (Rev. 2:20). In no uncertain terms,

He warns that if the church refuses to deal with the problem, "I will cast her [the prophetess] upon a bed of sickness, and those who commit adultery with her into great tribulation . . . and I will kill her children [those following her] with pestilence" (Rev. 2:22–23). So much for the popular notion that Jesus is a "meek and mild" fellow who is willing to tolerate sin!

In like manner, Jesus speaks sternly to the church at Laodicea, the church that is symbolic of the predominating church of the end times. He denounces the church's worldliness and apathy and then warns that if there is no repentance, "I will spit you out of My mouth" (Rev. 3:16).

The initial focus in Revelation on the sins of the Church and God's determination to deal with those sins forcibly, if necessary, is an illustration of what Peter meant when He wrote that judgment will "begin with the household of God; and if it begins with us first, what will be the outcome for those who do not obey the gospel of God?" (1 Pet. 4:17).

Revelation answers Peter's question by making it clear that God intends to unleash His wrath upon the world in unprecedented fury. He will deal with His Church first, even as He is doing today — revealing and purging corruption in both churches and ministries worldwide. But as Peter warned, and as Revelation reveals, the judgment falling upon the Church is nothing compared to the wrath that is going to be poured out on the world.

The truth of the matter is that the God of love, grace, and mercy that we hear about so much in Christian preaching and teaching is also a God of perfect holiness, righteousness, and justice. He is a God who does not tolerate unrepentant sin. He is a God who cannot be mocked or deceived (Gal. 6:7). He is a God who promises that our sins "will find us out" (Num. 32:23) and that "they who sow the wind, will reap the whirlwind" (Hos. 8:7).

John the Baptist declared in one of his sermons that God deals with sin in only one of two ways — either grace or wrath (John 3:36). That means that every person on earth is under either the grace of God or the wrath of God. It is a glorious thing to be under God's grace through faith in Jesus. It means your sins have been forgiven and forgotten and that the return of Jesus will be your "blessed hope" (Titus 2:13). It is a terrible thing to be under God's wrath, rejecting the love, grace, and mercy He has offered through Jesus. For such a person, the return of Jesus will be their holy terror. They will cry out to the rocks and mountains, "Fall on us and hide us from the presence of Him who sits on the throne [the Father], and from the wrath of the Lamb [Jesus]" (Rev. 6:16).

The Bible tells us that the Lord is "compassionate and gracious, slow to anger, and abounding in lovingkindness" — that He is willing to forgive iniquity, transgression, and sin when there is repentance (Exod. 34:6). But the Word makes it equally clear that "He will by no means leave the guilty [the unrepentant] unpunished" (Exod. 34:7). The prophet Nahum summed it up powerfully in the following statement:

> A jealous and avenging God is the Lord; The Lord is avenging and wrathful. The Lord takes vengeance on His adversaries, And He reserves wrath for His enemies. The Lord is slow to anger and great in power, And the Lord will by no means leave the guilty unpunished (Nah. 1:2–3).

This passage highlights a very important aspect of God's wrath that is not widely understood. He is slow to anger. He is not impetuous. And because He is patient, not wishing that any should perish (2 Pet. 3:9), He reserves His wrath, allowing it to build up over a long period of time before He unleashes it.

This characteristic of God in responding to sin is mentioned in Genesis 15. God told Abraham that his descendants would be taken captive into a foreign land and would have to stay there for four hundred years before He would allow them to return to Canaan (Gen. 15:13). He went on to explain that they could not return before that time because "the iniquity of the Amorite is not yet complete" (Gen. 15:16). In other words, the sins of the Amorites had to accumulate to a certain point before God would pour out His wrath upon them by allowing the Children of Israel to return and conquer them.

Daniel refers to this characteristic of God in the great prayer of repentance that he prayed for his nation of Israel during their captivity in Babylon. He refers to the fact that the Lord had not ignored their sins but had, instead "kept the calamity in store" and then brought it on them in His perfect timing (Dan. 9:14). Paul also mentions how God reserves wrath. He warns those who are living in rebellion against God that "because of your stubbornness and unrepentant heart, you are storing up wrath for yourself in the day of wrath and revelation of the righteous judgment of God" (Rom. 2:5).

In the physical realm there are laws of nature that produce immediate responses to our misdeeds. If you step off a roof, you will instantly fall to the ground. If you stick your hand in a fire, you will be burned immediately. God's spiritual laws do not work the same way. Violation of them may produce an instant sense of guilt, if the conscience is not seared. But other consequences may be delayed — even for years.

My colleague Dennis Pollock often illustrates this point by noting that when we sin, no hammer suddenly appears in the sky and then smacks us on the head. If it did, we would live by sight and not by faith. The usual situation is that we appear to get away with the sin. Our conscience — or the Holy Spirit within, if the person is a believer — will be calling us to repentance, but we can ignore conscience and stifle the Spirit. So, the embezzler keeps on taking money and the adulterer continues to engage in immorality.

But there is always a payday for sin — a day of reckoning. It may be delayed, but it is inevitable. King Solomon explained it this way. "Because the sentence against an evil deed is not executed quickly, therefore the hearts of the sons of men among them are given fully to do evil" (Eccles. 8:11). He then warns that people who persist in sin should fear God (Eccles. 8:12) because "God will bring every act to judgment, everything which is hidden, whether it is good or evil" (Eccles. 12:14).

Billy Graham has often said, "If God does not judge San Francisco, He is going to have to apologize to Sodom and Gomorrah!" I understand and share his feeling. Again, the only reason God has not yet poured out His wrath on San Francisco or America is because He does not wish that any should perish. Even in the midst of gross sin, He patiently awaits repentance. But in the meantime, He is storing up wrath.

Revelation presents the story of how God will unleash His awful wrath upon a rebellious, God-hating world. He will do so in a series of judgments so overwhelming that more than one-half of humanity and two-thirds of the Jews will be killed.

The Psalmist cries out, "O Lord, God of vengeance, shine forth! Rise up, O Judge of the earth; render recompense to the proud. . . . they have said, 'The Lord does not see, nor does the God of Jacob pay heed.' . . . The Lord our God will destroy them" (Ps. 94:1–23). In Revelation we hear an echo of these words before the throne of God in heaven as the spirits of Christian martyrs cry out, "How long, O Lord, holy and true, will You refrain from judging and avenging our blood on those who dwell on the earth?" (Rev. 6:10).

The Book of Revelation presents the answer to that question. Wrath is coming. The Christ-haters are going to receive justice. The redeemed are going to be vindicated. And when it occurs, all of heaven is going to shout, "Hallelujah! Salvation and glory and power belong to our God; because His judgments are true and righteous; for . . . He has avenged the blood of His bond-servants" (Rev. 19:1–2).

Jesus is coming soon, and He is coming to judge and wage war against the enemies of God (Rev. 19:11). He will "tread the wine press of the fierce wrath of God, the Almighty" (Rev. 19:15).

Humanity Is Corrupt to the Core

The religion of the world, masquerading under many different names, is humanism — the belief that man is basically good and capable of perfection. A corollary is that man is capable of saving himself through his good works.

Christianity is the only religion in the world that denies the satanic concept of salvation by good works. Here's how the apostle Paul put it: "For by grace you have been saved through faith; and that not of yourselves, it is a gift of God; not as a result of works, that no one should boast" (Eph. 2:8–9).

Christianity is also the only world religion that recognizes the inherent spiritual depravity of man. That's because the Scriptures clearly teach that man is born with a sin nature inherited from Adam, that man is basically evil in nature, and that man's only hope for true change is by spiritual renewal through faith in Jesus as Lord and Savior.

Concerning the nature of man, the Psalmist wrote, "There is no one who does good, not even one" (Ps. 14:3 and 53:1). In like manner, Isaiah wrote, "All of us like sheep have gone astray, each of us has turned to his own way" (Isa. 53:6). Jeremiah warns that we should trust only in the Lord and not in other people because "the heart is more deceitful than all else and is desperately sick" (Jer. 17:9). Paul says that people in their natural state are "by nature children of wrath" (Eph. 2:3). In Romans, Paul sums it all up powerfully in these words:

> There is none righteous, not even one;
> There is none who understands,
> There is none who seeks for God;
> All have turned aside, together they have become useless;
> There is none who does good,
> There is not even one (Rom. 3:10–12).

He then explains why this bleak portrayal of the human condition is true. He says "for all have sinned and fall short of the glory of God" (Rom. 3:23).

Because of the depraved nature of man, the Bible makes it equally clear that no person can save himself through good works. Isaiah declared that all our good works are like filthy rags before the Lord (Isa. 64:6). That's because righteous deeds can never atone for our sins. Only the blood of Jesus, a sinless man, can do that (Heb. 4:15 and 1 John 1:7).

This doesn't mean that good works are irrelevant. They are very relevant — but not to the determination of our eternal destiny. We are saved by grace through faith (Eph. 2:8). Our good works are relevant to our sanctification (being shaped into the image of Jesus). They are relevant to our participation in the advancement of the Lord's kingdom. And they relate to the special rewards that we will receive when we stand before the judgment seat of Jesus.

We don't work to be saved; we work because we are saved. Works are evidence of our salvation (James 2:14–26). Thus, even though Paul says point blank that we are saved by grace through faith, and not as a result of works (Eph. 2:8), he immediately adds that we are saved "for good works, which God prepared beforehand, that we should walk in them" (Eph. 2:10). In his letter to Titus, Paul states that the redeemed will be "zealous for good deeds" (Titus 2:14) and will be "careful to engage in good deeds" (Titus 3:8).

These basic biblical truths about the nature of man and salvation are strongly affirmed in the Book of Revelation. Concerning man's nature, Revelation presents a bleak picture from beginning to end. Instead of repenting in response to God's judgments during the Tribulation, we are told that the vast majority of people will shake their fists at God and curse Him:

> And the rest of mankind, who were not killed by these plagues, did not repent of the works of their hands, so as not to worship demons, and the idols of gold and of silver and of brass and of stone and of wood, which can neither see nor walk; and they did not repent of their murders nor of their sorceries nor of their immorality nor of their thefts (Rev. 9:20–21).

In Revelation 11 we are told that humanity will hate the two prophets in Jerusalem who will spend the first half of the

Tribulation calling the world to repentance. The hatred will be so intense that in the middle of the Tribulation, when the Antichrist kills the prophets, all the world will celebrate their deaths by exchanging gifts in a sort of satanic Christmas (Rev. 11:10).

As the judgments of the Tribulation continue, people's hearts seem to harden in their rebellion against God. In the midst of the third and final set of judgments (the bowl judgments), we are told that people will continue to blaspheme God and refuse to repent (Rev. 16:11).

But the saddest testimony about the nature of man that is contained in Revelation is to be found in chapter 20 regarding humanity's response to the millennial reign of Jesus. We are told that after 1,000 years of peace, righteousness, and justice, the majority of those born during that time will rise up in revolt and try to overthrow Jesus. This last revolt will demonstrate conclusively that you cannot alter the basic nature of people by changing their environment (one of the fundamental assumptions of humanism). Rather, the only way to truly change anyone is through the indwelling of the Holy Spirit which comes through faith in Jesus as Lord and Savior.

Revelation paints an equally grim picture about the humanistic concept that man can justify himself before God through good works. Chapter 20 concludes with the Great White Throne Judgment that will occur at the end of the Millennium (Rev. 20:11–15). All those who have ever lived and died outside a faith relationship with God will be resurrected and judged of their works to determine their eternal destiny. And since no one can be justified before God by their deeds, *all* who experience this judgment will be condemned to the "lake of fire," which is hell. The Great White Throne Judgment is a terrifying judgment of the damned. And the damned are those who have put their hope in their good works rather than Jesus.

Humanity Is Subject to Deception

Because of the fallen, sinful nature of man, we are all subject to deception. We are warned to "take heed lest we fall" (1 Cor. 10:12).

To protect us from deception, the Bible also warns us not to put our trust in people, and especially in political leaders (Ps. 118:8–9). We are also told that we should not even trust ourselves (Prov. 3:5). After all, self-deception is the worst form of deception.

These warnings are particularly appropriate for the day and age in which we now live because the Bible repeatedly states that the end times will be an age of widespread deception. In His Olivet Discourse, Jesus warned three times that false Christs and prophets would characterize the end times (Matt. 24:5, 11, 24). Some, He said, would even "show great signs and wonders" (Matt. 24:24). "See to it that no one misleads you," He warned (Matt. 24:4).

Paul showed a particular concern in his writings about the danger of deception. He warned that "savage wolves" will attack "the flock" [the Church] from within (Acts 20:29). He explained what he meant when he added, "From among your own selves men will arise, speaking perverse things, to draw away disciples after them" (Acts 20:30).

To the young preacher Timothy, Paul wrote, "The Spirit explicitly says that in later times some will fall away from the faith, paying attention to deceitful spirits and doctrines of demons" (1 Tim. 4:1). He also warned that a time would come when people would "not endure sound doctrine, but wanting to have their ears tickled, they will accumulate for themselves teachers in accordance to their own desires; and will turn away their ears from the truth, and will turn aside to myths" (2 Tim. 4:3–4).

The Book of Revelation makes it clear that these warnings are more than justified, for the Tribulation is going to be a period of intense deception. We are told that Satan will deceive the whole world as he works through the Antichrist and the false prophet (Rev. 12:9 and 20:10).

The Antichrist will rise to power in Europe through deception. As Daniel puts it, he will be "skilled in intrigue" (Dan. 8:23). The false prophet will deceive the world into worshiping the Antichrist. He will do this through signs and wonders, like making fire come down from heaven (Rev. 13:13–14). His ultimate deception will take place when he appears to give life to an image of the Antichrist (Rev. 13:15). At the end of the Millennium, Satan will be let loose for a season, and he will deceive the nations, gathering them to war against Jesus who will be ruling the world from Jerusalem (Rev. 20:8).

You may be thinking, *Satan could never deceive me.* If so, then you are living in pride, and you are a prime candidate for deception. I'm convinced that most people think they cannot be deceived because they expect deceivers to appear as blasphemous God-haters who can be easily detected. Satan is not that stupid. Keep in mind that the Scriptures warn us that "Satan disguises himself as an angel of light," and he disguises his disciples as "servants of righteousness" (2 Cor. 11:14–15).

How then are we to protect ourselves from deception? The Bible makes it clear. *We are to test everything by God's Word.* Test, test, test, and then test some more. That is our armor against deception. Paul warned that if he or an angel from heaven should preach a gospel contrary to that contained in the Scriptures, we are to reject it and the person is to be accursed (Gal. 1:8–9). Accordingly, Paul complimented the Bereans because they tested everything he taught them by "examining the Scriptures daily, to see whether these things were so" (Acts 17:10–11). And in his first letter to the church at Thessalonica, Paul exhorted them to "examine everything carefully" and to "hold fast to that which is good" (1 Thess. 5:21).

In like manner, in His letter to the church at Ephesus, Jesus complimented the saints there because they "put to the test those who call themselves apostles, and they are not, and you found them to be false" (Rev. 2:2).

Humanity Was Created for Worship

Some churches emphasize preaching. Others focus on communion. The biblical emphasis is upon worship, for man was created for fellowship with his Creator. Jesus emphasized this when He told the woman at the well in Samaria that "an hour is coming, and now is, when the true worshipers shall worship the Father in spirit and in truth; for such people the Father seeks to be His worshipers" (John 4:23).

This is the reason God hates idolatry with such a passion. The prohibition against idolatry was listed as the first of the Ten Commandments (Exod. 20:3). It is the sin that led to the downfall of King Solomon (1 Kings 11:1–8). It is the sin that produced the Babylonian captivity of the Jews (Ezek. 6:1–6). It is the sin that the apostle John warned the Church against in some of the last words he penned: "Little children, guard yourselves from idols" (1 John 5:21).

God desires intimacy with His creation, and He does not want to share that fellowship with false gods. That's why He proclaimed long ago that He is a "jealous and avenging God" (Nah. 1:2). God desires so much to bless us with His presence that He actively seeks worshipers! (John 4:23). And the Psalmist says that when He finds them, He inhabits their praises (Ps. 22:3). It is no wonder that we are exhorted over and over in the Scriptures to give ourselves to the Lord in worship. We are told to "give thanks to the Lord" (Ps. 92:1), to "sing for joy to the Lord" (Ps. 95:1), to "shout joyfully to the Lord" (Ps. 100:1), to "ascribe glory to the Lord" (Ps. 96:7), to "exalt the Lord" (Ps. 99:5), and to "worship at His footstool" (Ps. 99:5).

The New Testament contains many similar exhortations. The writer of Hebrews calls us to "continually offer up a sacrifice of praise to God, that is, the fruit of lips that give thanks to His name" (Heb. 13:15). Peter states that Christians are "living stones" who "are being built up as a spiritual house for holy priesthood, to offer up spiritual sacrifices acceptable to God through Jesus Christ" (1 Pet. 2:5). Paul sums it up by writing, "Rejoice always. Pray without ceasing," and "in everything give thanks" (1 Thess. 5:16–18).

The Book of Revelation confirms that our God is a God who relishes worship. Some of the greatest scenes of worship recorded in the Scriptures can be found in Revelation. When John is raptured to heaven to God's throne room (Rev. 4), he sees all the heavenly host caught up in worshiping the Father.

The "four living creatures" are singing about God's holiness, power, and eternal nature (Rev. 4:8). The 24 elders are bowing before the Lord's throne and are praising Him as Creator of all things (Rev. 4:10–11).

Later, in preparation for the completion of God's wrath in the pouring out of the bowl judgments, all the heavenly host break forth in song extolling the Lord for His "marvelous" works, His "righteous and true" ways, and His holiness (Rev. 15:3–4). When God's wrath is completed, heaven again breaks out in praise with a whole series of "Hallelujahs!" God is praised for His "glory and power," His "true and righteous" judgments, and His vengeance in behalf of martyred saints (Rev. 19:1–2).

Heaven appears to be filled with constant praise for who God is and for what He has done.

Revelation ends with a promise and a command pertaining to worship. The promise is that the redeemed will one day see the face of God (Rev. 22:4). This will occur when the eternal state begins on the new earth. This is a promise of incredible intimacy with our Creator. The command is given to John by an angel, and it applies to all believers. We are told that as we await the return of Jesus, we are to "worship God" (Rev. 22:9).

Satan Is Destined for Defeat

The Lord called me into the ministry when I was 20 years old. I said, "Lord, here am I, send anyone but me!" I ran from the Lord as hard as I could run for the next 20 years. When the Lord finally got my attention, and I decided to yield to His call on my life, I ran into a severe spiritual problem that kept me in a defeated state.

You see, every time I got up to teach or preach, Satan would get all over me, reminding me of my past sins. "Who are you to preach or teach God's Word?" he would ask. "Don't you remember when you did . . . ?" He would then run a litany of my sins before me in my memory. By the time he got finished with me, it was all I could do to open my mouth!

The Book of Revelation delivered me from this spiritual

torment when it clearly revealed what is going to happen to Satan. First, he is going to be cast down from heaven in the middle of the Tribulation (Rev. 12:9). When this happens, he will no longer be allowed to stand before God's throne and accuse the saints (Rev. 12:10–11). Then, at the end of the Tribulation when Jesus returns, Satan's Antichrist and false prophet will be seized and thrown into hell. Satan himself will be bound for the duration of the Lord's reign on earth.

At the end of Jesus' millennial reign, Satan will be let loose for a short period of time to deceive the nations, and then he will be thrown into hell to join the Antichrist and false prophet in everlasting torment (Rev. 20:10). Isaiah says that in the eternal state, the redeemed will be able to look upon Satan in his torment, and that he will appear so pitiful that they will ask in wonder, "Is this the man who made the earth tremble, who shook kingdoms, who made the world like a wilderness and overthrew its cities . . . ?" (Isa. 14:16–17).

Paul promised us that Satan will be "crushed" when Jesus returns (Rom. 16:20). Revelation affirms that promise. Because of that, when Satan now tries to remind me of my past, I remind him of his future, and he is the one who sulks away in defeat. Praise the Lord!

Jesus Is Destined to Triumph

The first time Jesus came, He suffered rejection and humiliation. He was spurned by both Jews and Gentiles. He was mocked, slandered, cursed, and crucified. He triumphed spiritually through the power of His glorious resurrection. He is destined to triumph physically when He returns in His glorified body to reign as King of kings over all the earth.

The Book of Revelation affirms the promise that Jesus will one day return to reign over all the nations of the world from Mount Zion in Jerusalem. When He returns, voices in heaven will shout, "The kingdom of the world has become the kingdom of our Lord, and of His Christ; and He will reign forever and ever" (Rev. 11:15). Although the initial purpose of His return will be to judge and wage war against the enemies of God (Rev. 19:11), his ultimate purpose will be to reign with a "rod of iron" as "King of kings and Lord of lords" (Rev. 19:15–16).

Revelation 20 tells us that He will reign for 1,000 years before the earth is destroyed by fire. Then, His eternal reign will continue on a new and perfected earth. Beyond stating the length of the Lord's reign on the current earth, Revelation 20 does not tell us much about His millennial reign. What will it be like? What will be its characteristics? We have to turn to the Old Testament prophets to find the details.

The greatest of the millennial prophets is Isaiah. He states that the Lord's reign will be worldwide (Isa. 2:2) and will be characterized by peace between the nations (Isa. 2:4). Righteousness and justice will abound (Isa. 9:7), and "the earth will be full of the knowledge of the Lord as the waters cover the sea" (Isa. 11:9). The glory and majesty of Jesus will be manifested before the nations (Isa. 24:23 and 35:2). Holiness will abound (Isa. 4:2–4), and the world will be captivated with an attitude of joy and praise (Isa. 35:10).

Israel will be restored as the prime nation of the world, and God's blessings will flow forth to the nations through Israel (Isa. 60–61 and Zeph. 3:19–20). Jerusalem will serve as the world's spiritual and political capital (Isa. 2:2–3 and 56:6–8). The city will be "a crown of beauty in the hand of the Lord" (Isa. 62:3), and the Lord will make the city "a praise in the earth" (Isa. 62:7).

All of nature will be reconciled to itself and to man. The wolf will lie down with the lamb. The lion will eat straw with the ox. Little children will play with lions and cobras (Isa. 11:6–9). Man will have dominion over nature and will no longer have to strive against nature to raise his food (Isa. 30:23–26).

Life spans for those in the flesh will be extended for the full length of the Millennium (Isa. 65:19–22). Disease will be curtailed (Isa. 33:24), and healing will be provided for mind and body (Isa. 29:18–19 and 32:3–4). There will be great prosperity. No one will be homeless or hungry (Isa. 65:21–23).

And Jesus will live in our midst, reigning in His glorified body. Jerusalem will be the place of His feet (Isa. 60:13). We will behold Him with our eyes (Isa. 30:20). He will be exalted (Isa. 52:13), and He will manifest His glory (Isa. 24:23, 35:2, 40:5 and 66:18).

There are many other prophecies about the Lord's millennial reign in the Old Testament. The Psalms are full of them, like the passage in Psalm 22 that says "the ends of the earth will remember and turn to the Lord, and all the families of the nations will worship before Him" (Ps. 22:27). Ezekiel presents a priestly view of the Millennium, describing the millennial temple in detail (Ezek. 40–46). Micah, God's prophet of social responsibility, provides us with a political view of the Millennium, emphasizing the peace and prosperity that will characterize the Lord's reign (Mic. 4:1–7).

Zechariah says the Messiah will come and dwell in the midst of the Jews in Jerusalem (Zech. 2:10 and 8:3). He adds that "many nations [the Gentiles] will join themselves to the Lord in that day" (Zech. 2:11). He further states that the Messiah will establish a theocracy in which He will reign both as a priest and king (Zech. 6:12–13). Jerusalem will be called "the City of Truth," and the Lord's kingdom will be referred to as "the Holy Mountain" (Zech. 8:3). God will protect Jerusalem as "a wall of fire around her," and He will be "the glory in her midst" (Zech. 2:5). In fact, Isaiah says that the Shekinah glory of God will hover over the city like a canopy, providing shelter (Isa. 4:5).

Joel and Ezekiel both proclaim that in that day the whole world will come to realize that the Lord Jesus is God (Joel 3:17 and Ezek. 6:7). Zephaniah says "The King of Israel, the Lord" will be "in your midst," and the whole world will realize that "the Lord your God is in your midst" (Zeph. 3:15, 17). Because the Lord will be living in Jerusalem and reigning from there, Ezekiel says that the official name of the city will be changed from Jerusalem to Yahweh-shemmah, meaning, "The Lord is there" (Ezek. 48:35).

These references are only a smattering of the hundreds

of prophecies in the Hebrew Scriptures about the future reign of the Messiah on this earth. The quaint but widespread idea that Revelation 20 is the only chapter of the Bible that mentions a future earthly reign of the Messiah is totally false.

The Redeemed Are Destined to Reign with Jesus

The Book of Revelation teaches that those of us who are saved by grace through faith in Jesus are going to share in His future earthly reign. Jesus himself promises this blessing in His letter to the church at Thyatira. He says to him who overcomes, "I will give authority over the nations; and he shall rule them with a rod of iron" (Rev. 2:26–27). In his letter to the church in Laodicea, Jesus repeats this promise: "He who overcomes, I will grant to him to sit down with Me on My throne, as I also overcame and sat down with My Father on His throne" (Rev. 3:21). The throne of Jesus is the throne of David (2 Sam. 7:8–16) which is located in Jerusalem (Ps. 122:1–5).

In chapter 5 of Revelation the 24 elders in heaven are pictured as singing a song praising Jesus for the redemption He has provided mankind (Rev. 5:9-10). In that song they state that the redeemed will reign in Jesus' kingdom "upon the earth." In Revelation 20:4 we see the fulfillment of that prophecy following Jesus' second coming when He allows those to whom "judgment was given" to reign with Him. As I pointed out earlier in my commentary on Revelation (chapter 2 of this book), those to whom judgment has been promised include Old Testament saints, the apostles, Church Age saints, and Tribulation martyrs.

The promise that the redeemed will reign with Jesus is not one that can be found only in the Book of Revelation. Speaking of the Millennium, Isaiah writes, "Behold, a king will reign righteously, and princes will rule justly" (Isa. 32:1). Daniel clarifies this statement when he reports that he had a "night vision" in which he saw God the Father giving "the Son of Man" dominion over all the earth (Dan. 7:13–14). He then adds, that "the saints of the Highest One will receive the kingdom and possess the kingdom" (Dan. 7:18). Elaborating this promise, he says, "Then the sovereignty, the dominion, and the greatness of all the kingdoms under the whole heaven will be given to the people of the saints of the Highest One" (Dan. 7:27). Paul reaffirms this promise to Church Age saints when he states, "If we endure, we shall also reign with Him" (2 Tim. 2:12).

There is just no way that anyone can successfully spiritualize these promises to mean that Jesus is currently reigning over the earth through His Church. All the nations of the world are in rebellion against Jesus, and the Church is being persecuted in all of them. Jesus is not reigning over the nations and neither is the Church. But a day of triumph is coming soon when Jesus returns. The kings and presidents will crawl into holes in the ground and cry out for rocks to fall on them (Isa. 2:19 and Rev. 6:15–16). The nations "will quake" at His presence (Isa. 64:1), and they will be subdued to His will as He begins to rule with a "rod of iron" (Ps. 2:7–9).

History Has Meaning, and There Is Hope for the World

The pagan view of history is that it is a meaningless cycle of events. The Book of Revelation screams "No!" to this concept.

Revelation affirms the thesis presented in Genesis, and reiterated throughout the Bible, that God has a master plan and that He has the wisdom and the power to see that plan through to consummation. It is a glorious plan of redemption that was hinted at in the Garden of Eden immediately after Adam and Eve sinned. God told them that He would one day provide redemption for their sin through "the seed of woman" (Gen. 3:15). The details of the plan were first revealed to Abraham when God made a covenant with him in which He promised that He would bless "all the families of the earth" through Abraham's descendants (Gen. 11:1–3).

This covenant was renewed to Abraham's son Isaac (Gen. 26:1-5), and to his son Jacob (Gen. 28:3–4). Jacob's name was later changed to Israel, and the covenant was renewed to his descendants who came to be known as "the children of Israel"

(Ps. 105:8–11). Through these people God supplied both His Word and the Messiah, Jesus of Nazareth.

Jesus shed His blood on the cross as a sacrifice of atonement for the sins of mankind, making it possible for those who place their faith in Him to be forgiven and reconciled to God the Father. Upon this truth, Jesus established His church and commissioned it to go forth to all the world and preach the good news of salvation by grace through faith in Him.

He also proclaimed that He would one day return to this earth to bring history to its climax by pouring out the wrath of God upon those who have rejected God's grace and love, and by establishing a kingdom that would subdue the nations and flood the earth with peace, righteousness, and justice.

The Book of Revelation begins with Jesus' bold proclamation that He is "the first and the last," the One who has overcome death and will live forevermore (Rev. 1:17–18). In other words, Jesus is the beginning and end of history, and He is the meaning of history.

Genesis teaches that history had a definite beginning when God created the heavens and the earth, the plant and animal kingdoms, and mankind. Revelation reveals that history will also have a definite ending.

The world as we know it will come to a screeching halt when Jesus returns to reign. Politics as usual will come to an end. Social injustice will cease. Iniquity will give way to righteousness. Despair will be converted into hope. Sadness will be replaced with joy. The Lord will provide "a garland instead of ashes, the oil of gladness instead of mourning, the mantle of praise instead of a spirit of fainting" (Isa. 61:3).

And then, at the end of the Lord's millennial reign, this earth will be consumed in fire and reshaped into a perfected new earth where the redeemed will dwell eternally in glorified bodies inside a New Jerusalem in the presence of the Father and the Son. Think of it — everything we value and hold dear in this present world will ultimately be consumed in fire (2 Pet. 3:10–13 and Rev. 21:1).

All the wealth and honors this world has to offer will

become ashes. The only thing of eternal importance will be the decision we made, or did not make, in this life regarding Jesus. That decision will determine our eternal destiny, whether heaven or hell.

The Crucial Question

The one thing that matters most in this life is how each of us answer the question that the Roman governor Pilate presented to the lynch mob when Jesus was arrested. He asked, "What shall I do with Jesus who is called the Christ?" (Matt. 27:22).

Will you turn your back on Him, ignore the warnings of Revelation, and end up being condemned at the Great White Throne Judgment? Will you chose the lake of fire — hell — as your destiny?

Or will you humble yourself, confess your sins, and put your faith in Jesus as your Lord and Savior? To do so means that you will become an overcomer who is an heir of all the blessings of God that are promised in Revelation: "He who overcomes shall inherit these things, and I will be his God and he will be My son" (Rev. 21:7).

Which will it be for you? Glory or wrath? Life or death? My prayer is that you will chose life — eternal life in fellowship with your Creator. You can do so by humbly and sincerely praying this prayer:

Heavenly Father, I confess to You that I am a sinner. I am sorry for my sins, and I ask You to forgive me and save me as I put my faith in Your Son, Jesus, accepting Him as my Lord and Savior. In Jesus' name I pray. Amen.

If you prayed that prayer, seek out a fellowship of believers where the Word is taught and Jesus is exalted. Confess your new faith before them and manifest it in water baptism. And then get involved in the life of that church so that you can begin to grow spiritually and you can begin to use your gifts to expand the Lord's kingdom.

If you are already a child of God but have grown cold in your faith, please pray this prayer:

> Heavenly Father, I confess that I have taken my eyes off Jesus and have grown cold in my faith. Forgive me, Father, and renew me through your Holy Spirit. Keep me grounded in daily study of Your Word and in daily prayer. Enable me to reach my full potential in You, allowing You to live Your life through me. May I be a Spirit-filled vessel for You to work through to touch others for Your precious Son, Jesus, in whose name I pray. Amen.

Jesus left us with a wonderful promise. His last words on this earth, recorded in Revelation 22:20, were "Yes, I am coming quickly." The apostle John cried out in response, "Amen. Come, Lord Jesus!" Let us cherish the Lord's promise just as John did. Let us commit our lives to holiness and evangelism as we await the Lord's return. And let us cry out daily from the depths of our hearts, "Maranatha! Come quickly, Lord Jesus!" (1 Cor. 16:22).

Endnotes

Chapter 1 — Understanding Revelation

1. For a detailed development of the challenge of societal decay and apostasy in the Church and how Christians should respond to both, see the author's book, *Living for Christ in the End Times* (Green Forest, AR: New Leaf Press, 2000).

2. Henry Morris, *The Revelation Record* (Wheaton, IL: Tyndale House Publishers, 1983), p. 25.

3. C. I. Scofield, *Scofield Study Bible: NIV Readers Edition* (Oxford, England: Oxford University Press, 1989).

4. For an excellent presentation of four ways to interpret Revelation (historicist, preterist, futurist, and spiritual), see *Revelation: Four Views, A Parallel Commentary*, Steve Gregg, editor (Nashville, TN: Thomas Nelson Publishers, 1997).

5. LeRoy Edwin Froom, *The Prophetic Faith of Our Fathers*, Vol. I (Washington, DC: Review and Herald Press, 1950), p. 205–308.

6. Ibid., p. 215–216.

7. Ibid., p. 241–267, 352–361.

8. Ibid., p. 233–234.

9. Ibid., p. 473–491.

10. Leroy Edwin Froom, *The Prophetic Faith of Our Fathers*, Vol. II (Washington, DC: Review and Herald Press, 1948), p. 241–282.

11. Most of the commentaries of the 19th century interpreted Revelation from the historicist viewpoint. These include Albert Barnes, Adam Clarke, and Matthew Henry. For more information about this viewpoint, see the website of the Historicism Research Foundation — http://www. historicist.com.

12. James Luther Mays, editor, *Revelation in Interpretation: A Bible Commentary for Preaching and Teaching*, article by M. Eugene Boring, (Louisville, KY: John Knox Press, 1989), p. 49.

13. The website of Irvin Baxter Jr.'s ministry, End Time Ministries, is located at http://www.endtime.com.

14. For a good discussion of the preterist viewpoint, see Thomas Ice's article, "The Use of 'At Hand' in the Book of Revelation," *Futurist Foundations*, Vol. 1, No. 2, Aug–Sept 1994, published by the Pre-Trib Research Center.

15. Luis de Alcazar, *Rev. Patris Ludovici ab Alcasar . . . Vestigatio Arcani Sensus in Apocalypsi* (Antverpiae: Apud Ioannem Keerbergium, 1614).

16. The foremost exponent of the radical preterist viewpoint is Kenneth Gentry. See, for example, his book, *The Beast of Revelation* (Tyler, TX: Institute for Christian Economics, 1989).

17. A good example of the extreme preterist viewpoint can be found in the book by Max R. King, *The Spirit of Prophecy* (Warren, OH: Parkman Road Church of Christ, 1971).

18. William Milligan, *The Book of Revelation* (London: Hodder and Stoughton, 1889).

19. Gregg, *Revelation: Four Views, A Parallel Commentary*, p. 43.

20. William Hendricksen, *More Than Conquerors: An Interpretation of the Book of Revelation* (Grand Rapids, MI: Baker Book House, 1939), p. 43.

Chapter 2 — Interpreting Revelation

1. Froom, *The Prophetic Faith of Our Fathers*, Vol. I, p. 101–104.

2. John Stott, *Basic Introduction to the New Testament* (Grand Rapids, MI: William B. Eerdmans, revised edition 1986), p. 173–174.

3. Hal Lindsey, *There's a New World Coming* (Santa Ana, CA: Vision House Publishers, 1973), p. 138–139.

4. Richard N. Ostling, "A Summit for Peace in Assisi," *Time*, November 10, 1986, p. 78–79.

5. Vatican City (RNS), "Pope Says Unbelievers Will Be Saved If They Live a Just Life," December 6, 2000.

Chapter 3 — Systematizing Revelation

1. Paul L. Maier, translator and editor, *Josephus: The Essential Works* (Grand Rapids, MI: Kregel Publications, 1988), p. 210.

2. Hans Volkmann, "Antiochus IV, Epiphanes," *Encyclopædia Britannica,* CD 99.

3. Maier, *Josephus: the Essential Works,* p. 368–372.

4. Froom, *The Prophetic Faith of Our Fathers*, Vol. I, p. 309–324.

5. Ibid., p. 651–655.

Chapter 4 — Probing Revelation

1. Froom, *The Prophetic Faith of Our Fathers*, Vol. I, p. 102–103, and 243–252.

2. Tim LaHaye, *Revelation Illustrated and Made Plain* (Grand Rapids, MI: Zondervan Publishing House, 1973), p. 190–203.

3. Marvin Rosenthal, *The Pre-Wrath Rapture of the Church* (Nashville, TN: Thomas Nelson Publishers, 1990).

4. Tim LaHaye and Jerry B. Jenkins, *Left Behind* (Wheaton, IL: Tyndale House Publishers, 1995), p. 37, 211.
5. Ibid., p. 211.
6. *Holy Bible, New Living Translation* (Wheaton, IL: Tyndale House Publishers, 1996).
7. LaHaye and Jenkins, *Left Behind*, p.214.
8. Ibid., p. 8.
9. Ibid., p. 300.
10. Ibid., p. 113.
11. Ibid., p. 232–233, 310–311.
12. Ibid., p. 456–457.
13. Ibid., p. 458.
14. Tim LaHaye and Jerry B. Jenkins, *Soul Harvest* (Wheaton, IL: Tyndale House Publishers, 1998), p. 86.
15. Ibid., p. 86.
16. Tim LaHaye and Jerry B. Jenkins, *Assassins* (Wheaton, IL: Tyndale House Publishers, 1999), p. 410–411.
17. Tim LaHaye and Jerry B. Jenkins, *The Indwelling* (Wheaton, IL: Tyndale House Publishers, 2000), p. 364–366.
18. LaHaye and Jenkins, *Left Behind*, p. 352.
19. Tim LaHaye and Jerry B. Jenkins, *Apollyon* (Wheaton, IL: Tyndale House Publishers, 1999), p. 259.
20. Charles Dyer with Angela Elwell Hunt, *The Rise of Babylon* (Wheaton, IL: Tyndale House, 1991).
21. LaHaye and Jenkins, *Left Behind*, p. 301–302.
22. Froom, *The Prophetic Faith of Our Fathers*, Vol. I, p. 257, 278.
23. Ibid., p. 554–555.
24. LaHaye and Jenkins, *Soul Harvest*, p. 172.

Prophecy Study Resources

One of the best overall books on Bible prophecy that has ever been published is *Things to Come* by Dwight Pentecost (Grand Rapids, MI: Zondervan, 1964). It is scholarly and comprehensive, written for serious, college-level students.

Surveys

The Master Plan, by David Reagan (Eugene, OR: Harvest House, 1993) contains a comprehensive survey of all aspects of Bible prophecy. It was written for the layman and is easy to read and understand. A similar comprehensive study that is more scholarly in its approach is a book by Paul N. Benware entitled *Understanding End Time Prophecy* (Chicago, IL: Moody Press, 1995).

With regard to end-time prophecies only, one of the best surveys for the more general reader is Leon Woods' book, *The Bible and Future Events* (Grand Rapids, MI: Zondervan, 1973). Other very readable surveys are *The Final Chapter* by S. Maxwell Coder (Wheaton, IL: Tyndale House, 1984) and *A Survey of Bible Prophecy* by R. Ludwigson (Grand Rapids, MI: Zondervan, 1973). *The King is Coming* by H.L. Willmington (Wheaton, IL: Tyndale House, 1973) presents an overview of end-time events in a very unique and easy-to-follow outline form.

A spiral-bound study guide by David Reagan called *The Christ in Prophecy Study Guide* (McKinney, TX: Lamb & Lion Ministries, 2001) presents an analytical survey of all messianic prophecy contained in both the Old and New Testaments. Another indispensable reference volume that presents an exhaustive survey is *All the Messianic Prophecies of the Bible* by Herbert Lockyer (Grand Rapids, MI: Zondervan, 1979).

A survey book intended for the serious student is Arnold Fruchtenbaum's encyclopedic study of Tribulation events which bears the strange title, *The Footsteps of the Messiah* (Tustin, CA: Ariel Press, 1982). It focuses on showing the sequence of end-time events and their relationship to each other.

A brief and fascinating survey book full of penetrating insights is one titled *What on Earth is God Doing?* (Neptune, NJ: Loizeaux Brothers, 1973). It was written by Renald Showers, a gifted teacher and writer who serves the Friends of Israel Ministry. The book presents a capsule overview of God's purposes in history from start to finish.

Interpretation

Nothing is more important to the understanding of Bible prophecy than the principles of interpretation that are applied to it. An excellent introductory book for the general reader is *How to Study Bible Prophecy for Yourself* by Tim LaHaye (Eugene, OR: Harvest House, 1990).

The most profound book ever written on the topic is *The Interpretation of Prophecy* by Paul Lee Tan (Winona Lake, IN: Assurance Publishers, 1974). This book is an essential tool for any serious student of prophecy.

The history of prophetic interpretation is presented in great detail in the amazing, four-volume, encyclopedic study called *The Prophetic Faith of Our Fathers*, edited by LeRoy Edwin Froom (Washington, DC: Review and Herald Press). Volume 1 (1950) covers the Early Church. Volume 2 (1948) surveys the Pre-Reformation and Reformation periods. Volume 3 (1946) looks at the Colonial American and European awakening. Volume 4 (1946) provides a look at the 19th century. This great work of scholarship took years to complete. The first two volumes are based upon original research conducted throughout Europe in the 1920s and 1930s, utilizing ancient documents, many of which were destroyed in World War II.

Symbolic

Perhaps the least understood area of prophecy is symbolic prophecy, sometimes called prophecy in type. About half of Herbert Lockyer's book *All the Messianic Prophecies of the Bible* is dedicated to this important topic (Grand Rapids, MI: Zondervan, 1979).

Two books concerning symbolic prophecy that are easy

to read and are full of useful insights are *Christ in the Tabernacle* by Louis Talbot (Chicago, IL: Moody Press, 1978) and *Jesus in the Feasts of Israel* by Richard Booker (S. Plainfield, NJ: Bridge Publishing, 1987).

Old Testament Prophets

A magnificent introduction to all the Old Testament prophets is provided by Leon Wood in his exceptional book *The Prophets of Israel* (Schaumburg, IL: Regular Baptist Press, 1979).

One of the finest commentators on the Old Testament prophets is Charles Feinberg, a messianic Jew. His works include *God Remembers: A Study of Zechariah* (Portland, OR: Multnomah Press, 1965); *Jeremiah: A Commentary* (Grand Rapids, MI: Zondervan, 1982); and *The Prophecy of Ezekiel: The Glory of the Lord* (Chicago, IL: Moody Press, 1969). A good introduction to Isaiah can be found in the book by Herbert Wolf entitled *Interpreting Isaiah: The Suffering and Glory of the Messiah* (Grand Rapids, MI: Zondervan, 1985).

An outstanding series of scholarly commentaries on Isaiah, Jeremiah, and Ezekiel can be found in volume 6 of *The Expositor's Bible Commentary* edited by Frank E. Gaebelein (Grand Rapids, MI: Zondervan, 1986). The commentary on Isaiah is by G. W. Grogan; Jeremiah is by Charles L. Feinberg; and Ezekiel is by Ralph H. Alexander.

There are a number of good books about the Minor Prophets. Two that are designed for the general reader are *Major Truths from the Minor Prophets* by John Hunter (Grand Rapids, MI: Zondervan, 1977) and *Will We Ever Catch Up with the Bible?* by David Hubbard (Glendale, CA: Regal Books, 1977).

The best scholarly resource on the Minor Prophets is to be found in volume 7 of *The Expositor's Bible Commentary*, edited by Frank E. Gaebelein (Grand Rapids, MI: Zondervan, 1985). The authors of the commentaries on the specific books read like a "who's who" of evangelical scholars. A fine single volume scholarly study is the one by Charles Feinberg entitled *The Minor Prophets* (Chicago, IL: Moody Press, 1976).

Israel

The best panoramic survey of Israel in prophecy is contained in Walter K. Price's intriguing book *Next Year in Jerusalem* (Chicago, IL: Moody Press, 1975). Another very good overview is Richard Booker's outstanding study, *Blow the Trumpet in Zion* (Tulsa, OK: Victory House, 1985).

An excellent book that relates prophecy to the history of Israel, particularly modern history, is called *It is No Dream* (W. Collingswood, NJ: The Spearhead Press, 1978). It was written by Elwood McQuaid, the director of the Friends of Israel Ministry. Charles Feinberg has also produced an excellent volume that mixes prophecy with history. It is titled *Israel: At the Center of History and Revelation* (Portland, OR: Multnomah Press, 1980).

Daniel

An outstanding verse-by-verse commentary on Daniel is the one by Leon Woods that is simply entitled *A Commentary on Daniel* (Grand Rapids, MI: Zondervan, 1973). The best one for the general reader is by Renald Showers. It is titled *The Most High God* (W. Collingswood, NJ: The Friends of Israel, 1982). A lighter book that is both fun to read and inspirational in character is *Daniel: God's Man in a Secular Society* by Donald Campbell (Grand Rapids, MI: Discovery House, 1988). It is designed to serve as a study guide for Bible study groups.

No book of the Bible has been attacked as viciously by theological liberals as the Book of Daniel. A tremendous defense of the book's integrity can be found in a volume called *Daniel in the Critic's Den* by Josh McDowell (San Bernardino, CA: Campus Crusade for Christ, 1979).

Revelation

Many excellent studies have been published about the Book of Revelation. For the general reader, the two best are *Revelation Illustrated and Made Plain* by Tim LaHaye (Grand Rapids, MI: Zondervan, 1973) and *There's a New World Com-*

ing by Hal Lindsey (Santa Ana, CA: Vision House, 1973). Lindsey's book is the best one he has ever written.

For those who desire to dig deeper, *The Revelation Record* (Wheaton, IL: Tyndale House, 1983) by Henry Morris presents a detailed verse-by-verse analysis. Dr. Morris is the distinguished founder of the Institute for Creation Research.

A very unique study of Revelation is the one produced by Salem Kirban, a born-again Arab. The book utilizes hundreds of photos, charts, and drawings to visually present the message of Revelation. It is titled *Revelation Visualized* (Huntingdon Valley, PA: Salem Kirban, Inc., 1978). What makes it even more unusual is that it is co-authored by Gary Cohen, a born-again Jew!

An outstanding introduction to Revelation and the various methods of interpreting it is supplied by Merrill Tenney in his remarkably balanced volume, *Interpreting Revelation* (Grand Rapids, MI: Eerdmans, 1957).

Millennial Viewpoints

The best introduction to the various and often confusing viewpoints of end-time prophecy is a book by Robert Lightner called *The Last Days Handbook* (Nashville, TN: Thomas Nelson, 1990).

A very thought-provoking book on the topic is one edited by Robert G. Clouse entitled *The Meaning of the Millennium* (Downer's Grove, IL: Inter-Varsity Press, 1977). It contains four viewpoints presented by advocates of those viewpoints. A similar but more detailed presentation of the four viewpoints can be found in the parallel commentary by Steve Gregg called *Revelation: Four Views* (Nashville, TN: Thomas Nelson, 1997). A scholarly presentation and analysis of the various views is contained in John Walvoord's book *The Millennial Kingdom.* (Grand Rapids, MI: Zondervan, 1959).

For a classic presentation of the fundamentals of premillennial theology, the book to read is *The Basis of the Premillennial Faith* by Charles Ryrie (Neptune, NJ: Loizeaux

Brothers, 1953). It is brief and incisive, and it is written with an irenic spirit.

The Antichrist

One of the most detailed studies of the Antichrist ever written is the book by Arthur W. Pink entitled *The Antichrist*. It is thoroughly biblical and very thought-provoking. It was originally published in 1923 but has been recently republished (Grand Rapids, MI: Kregel, 1988). The best current-day study is the book by Ed Hindson entitled *Is the Antichrist Alive and Well?: Ten Keys to His Identity* (Eugene, OR: Harvest House, 1998).

The Rapture

The important controversy over the timing of the Rapture has been best addressed by John Walvoord in two of his books: *The Blessed Hope and the Tribulation* (Grand Rapids, MI: Zondervan, 1976) and *The Rapture Question* (Grand Rapids, MI: Zondervan, 1979). Walvoord is the former president of Dallas Theological Seminary. Another fine book on the topic is *The Rapture* by Hal Lindsey (New York, NY: Bantam Books, 1983).

Tim LaHaye has written a very powerful and exhaustive defense of the Pre-Tribulation Rapture entitled *No Fear of the Storm: Why Christians Will Escape All the Tribulation* (Sisters, OR: Multnomah, 1992, later re-published as *Rapture Under Attack,* 1998).

Signs of the Times

This is a field that attracts many sensationalist writers. There is an abundance of books, but few good ones. One of the most fascinating is *World War III: Signs of the Impending Battle of Armageddon* by John Wesley White (Grand Rapids, MI: Zondervan, 1977).

A volume that is comprehensive in scope but exceptionally brief is *Signs of the Second Coming* by Robert G. Witty (Nashville, TN: Broadman Press, 1969). A more recent study, and an excellent one, is by Henry Morris. It is titled *Creation and the Second Coming* (Green Forest, AR: Master Books, 1991).

One of the best prophetic writers to emerge in recent years is Ed Hindson of Liberty University. His books are solidly biblical and down-to-earth, readable by the average Christian. He has written two outstanding studies of the signs of the times: *Final Signs* (Eugene, OR: Harvest House, 1996) and *Earth's Final Hour: Are We Really Running Out of Time?* (Eugene, OR: Harvest House, 1999). Another excellent writer in the field of Bible prophecy is Dave Hunt of Berean Ministries. He has produced a very insightful study of the end-time signs in his book *How Close Are We?* (Eugene, OR: Harvest House, 1993).

Heaven

The eternal state has been the most ignored area of Bible prophecy, probably because the Bible says so little about it. The best book on the topic — one that covers death, resurrection, and eternity — is *The Future Life* by Frenchman Rene Pache, translated into English by Helen Needham (Chicago, IL: Moody Press, 1962). A very worthwhile, exhaustive study of the eternal state can be found in Bob Chambers' book, *Heaven* (Joplin, MO: College Press, 1991). This is an unusual book because Chambers is an amillennialist who spiritualizes the prophecies about the Millennium while interpreting the prophecies about heaven literally!

Children

Only one book has ever been written for pre-school and elementary children concerning end-time prophetic events. It was written by David Reagan and is entitled *Jesus is Coming Again!* (Eugene, OR: Harvest House, 1992). The book emphasizes the positive promises of God regarding the Millennium and the eternal state.

Media

Dave Reagan and Chuck Missler have both produced cassette tape albums that contain verse-by-verse commentaries on the Book of Revelation. Reagan's *Revelation Overview*

(Lamb & Lion Ministries) contains 12 tapes. Missler's *Revelation Commentary* (Koinonia Ministries) consists of three albums with eight tapes each. Jack Van Impe has produced an excellent series of video commentaries on Revelation called *Revelation Revealed* (Jack Van Impe Ministries).

Ray Stedman's outstanding commentary on Revelation can be found posted on the Internet in 23 messages at www.pbc.org/stedman (Peninsula Bible Church).

The best illustrations of Revelation have been produced by Pat Marvenko Smith. She has illustrated every main scene of the book and has made the pictures available in a variety of forms — slides, posters, overhead transparencies, video, and PowerPoint (Revelation Illustrated Ministries).

Fiction

The "Left Behind" series of books by Tim LaHaye and Jerry B. Jenkins present a fictionalized story about the Rapture and the Tribulation that is based upon biblical prophecies. This series is published by Tyndale House and has broken all sales records for prophetic books. The series of novels has become a best seller even when compared to secular books. The books have been made available on audio tape, and special edited versions have been published for teens. The first of the volumes, entitled *Left Behind,* was published in 1995.

Bibles

The very first study Bible ever published came out in 1909. It is still one of the best-selling study Bibles in the world. It was produced by a Dallas pastor named C.I. Scofield and is called *The Scofield Study Bible* (Urichsville, OH: Barbour Publishing, 2000). It has been revised and updated regularly over the years by an editorial committee representing a premillennial, pre-tribulational viewpoint.

A newer study Bible that presents the same view of the passages related to end-time prophecy is *The Ryrie Study Bible* (Chicago, IL: Moody Press, 1976). Both the Scofield and Ryrie commentaries are available in a variety of translations. The latest and most up-to-date study Bible that focuses on the interpretation of prophecy is *The Tim LaHaye Prophecy Study Bible* (Chattanooga, TN: AMG Publishers, 2000).

The Living Bible Paraphrased (Wheaton, IL: Tyndale House, 1971), though not a typical study Bible, is nonetheless an interpretive Bible that reflects a premillennial interpretation of all key prophetic passages.

Classics

The greatest and most enduring classic on the return of Jesus is William E. Blackstone's book *Jesus Is Coming*. It was written in 1878. The third revised edition of 1908 has been recently re-published with an introduction by John Walvoord (Grand Rapids, MI: Kregel, 1989).

A foreign book that has come to be considered one of the great classics of end-time prophecy is *The Return of Jesus Christ* by Rene Pache, translated into English by William S. LaSor (Chicago, IL: Moody Press, 1955). It is must reading for any Bible prophecy enthusiast.

The 20th century American classic is, of course, Hal Lindsey's book *The Late Great Planet Earth* (Grand Rapids, MI: Zondervan, 1970). The *New York Times* has certified that it was the number one best-selling book in the world (with the exception of the Bible) for ten years, between 1970 and 1980!

Perhaps the most unusual book ever published on Bible prophecy is *Dispensational Truth* by Clarence Larkin (Philadelphia, PA: Reverend Clarence Larkin Estate, 1920). Larkin was a draftsman who devoted his talents to illustrating prophetic concepts with fascinating charts and diagrams. This is a classic that will keep you up all night!

Recommended Prophecy Ministries

All of the ministries listed below offer excellent study resources on the Book of Revelation as well as end-time prophecy in general. All the ministries are premillennial and pre-tribulational in their basic prophetic concepts.

According to Prophecy Ministries — Don Perkins
P.O. Box 6, Lemon Grove, CA 91946
phone: (619) 443-4038
email: atpro4se@millennianet.com
website: http://millennianet.com/atpro4se
The only Black evangelist in America who devotes full time to the teaching and preaching of Bible prophecy. Very balanced ministry with an outstanding website and many good study aids.

Ariel Ministries — Arnold Fruchtenbaum
P.O. Box 3723, Tustin, CA 92781
phone: (714) 259-4800
email: homeoffice@ariel.org
website: www.ariel.org
Messianic ministry with a strong emphasis on Bible prophecy. Conducts in-depth tours of Israel and produces many publications, tapes, and books.

Biblical Faith Ministries — Elbert and Sam Peak
P.O. Box 2, Abilene, TX 76904
phone: 1-800-639-0169
email: peak@propheticround-up.com
website: www.propheticround-up.com
Produces a television program with emphasis on Bible prophecy, and publishes a magazine called *The Prophetic Round-Up*. Conducts tours to Israel.

Christian Jew Foundation — Gary Hedrick
P.O. Box 345, San Antonio, TX 78292
phone: (210) 226-0421
email: orderline@cjf.org
website: www.cjf.org
     Messianic ministry with one of the oldest continually
broadcast radio programs. Presents a strong emphasis on Bible
prophecy in its many tapes and publications.

David Allen Lewis Ministry — David Lewis
P.O. Box 14444, Springfield, MO 65814
phone: 1-800-772-5687
email: aslansteward@davidallenlewis.com
website: www.davidallenlewis.com
     The evangelist is a renowned speaker and writer, focus-
ing on the Middle East and Israel.

Focus on Jerusalem Ministry — Darrell G. Young
901 Oatfield Road, Harrodsburg, KY 40330
phone: (859) 734-9056
email: young@kycom.net
website: www.focusonjerusalem.com
     Provides a monthly newsletter and website which follow
events in Israel, relating them to Bible prophecy.

Friends of Israel Gospel Ministry — Elwood McQuaid
P.O. Box 908, Bellmawr, NJ 08099
phone: 1-800-257-7843
email: foi@foigm.org
website: www.foigm.org
     Publishes an outstanding magazine called *Israel My
Glory*. Provides many tapes, videos, and publications that relate to Bible prophecy. Produces a nationally broadcast radio
program. Conducts tours to Israel. Operates an Institute of
Jewish Studies which offers both class work and correspondence courses.

God's News Behind the News — Ray Brubaker
P.O. Box 10475, St. Petersburg, FL 33733
phone: 1-800-366-1463
email: mail@godsnews.com
website: www.godsnews.com
Provides a bi-monthly magazine and a weekly television broadcast. Sponsors a large national conference yearly.

Grant R. Jeffrey Ministries — Grant Jeffrey
P.O. Box 129, Station U, Toronto, Ontario M8Z 5M4
phone: 1-800-711-1976
email: from website
website: www.grantjeffrey.com
Canadian ministry that focuses on book publishing.

Hal Lindsey Ministries — Hal Lindsey
P.O. Box 50097, Long Beach, CA 90815
phone: 1-800-TITUS-35
email: from website
website: hallindseyoracle.com
Website contains up-to-the-minute news reports from all over the world, written from a biblical and prophetic perspective. Many prophecy study resources available through the website.

Jack Van Impe Ministries — Jack Van Impe
P.O. Box 7004, Troy, MI 48007
phone: (288) 852-2244
email: jvimi@jvim.com
website: www.jvim.com
Produces a nationally broadcast television program, a bi-monthly magazine, and a monthly newsletter. Also produces a great variety of excellent video programs.

Koinonia House — Chuck Missler
P.O. Box D, Coeur d'Alene, ID 83816
phone: 1-800-546-8731
email: from website
website: www.khouse.org
    Daily radio program and monthly newsletter. Produces books and excellent cassette tape programs.

Lamb & Lion Ministries — David Reagan
P.O. Box 919, McKinney, TX 75070
phone: (972) 736-3567
email: lamblion@lamblion.com
website: www.lamblion.com
    Nationally broadcast radio program called "Christ in Prophecy." Produces extensive cassette tape programs, publishes a bi-monthly magazine, and conducts tours to Israel. Also produces video tape programs.

Lion of Judah Ministries — Gary Fisher
P.O. Box 681505, Franklin, TN 37068
phone: (615) 591-8036
email: garyf@nashville.com
website: http://sxws.com/LIONJUDH
    Monthly teaching newsletter. Focuses on conducting meetings and conferences.

Maranatha Evangelistic Ministries — Al Gist
224 Al Gist Road, Longville, LA 70652
phone (337) 725-6209
email: al_gist@hotmail.com
    Holds meetings with an emphasis on Bible prophecy as a tool of evangelism. Publishes a monthly newsletter that focuses on Israel in prophecy.

Midnight Call Ministries — Arno Froese
P.O. Box 280008, Columbia, SC 29228
phone: (803) 755-0733
email: info@midnightcall.com
website: www.midnightcall.com
    Publishes a monthly magazine that is distributed world-wide in many languages. Heavily involved in book publishing and sponsorship of prophetic conferences.

Pre-Trib Study Group — Tommy Ice
P.O. Box 14111, Arlington, TX 76094
phone: (817) 861-9199
email: icet@lwol.com
website: No website for the ministry, but many of the group's papers can be found on the website of According to Prophecy: http://millennianet.com/atpro4se/pretri2.html.
    The group's membership consists of most of the premillennial, pre-tribulational preachers, teachers, and college professors in America. It meets annually to discuss Bible prophecy issues and usually conducts a prophecy conference in conjunction with the meeting. Publishes a monthly newsletter.

Prophecy Central — Ron Graff
8166 Vinmar Ct., Alta Loma, CA 91701
phone: (909) 989-3119
email: ron@bible-prophecy.com
website: www.bible-prophecy.com
    An Internet ministry with extensive resources on-line. Also provides an exhaustive list of links to other prophetic ministries.

Prophecy in the News — J. R. Church
P.O. Box 7000, Moore, OK 73153
phone: (405) 634-1234
email: from the website
website: www.prophecyinthenews.com
    Presents multi-media programs, produces a television program, and publishes a magazine.

Prophetic Witness Movement International — Alec Passmore
P.O. Box 109, Leyland, Lancashire PR5 3GL, England
phone: 011-44-1772-452-846
email: info@pwmi.org
website: www.pwmi.org
   Founded in 1917 by F.B. Meyer in response to the Balfour
Declaration. Publishes a monthly magazine and conducts
meetings and conferences throughout Great Britain.

Prophezine — Bob Lally
unlisted address in Schenectady, New York
phone: unlisted
email: bob@prophezine.com
website: prophezine.com
   An excellent Internet magazine on Bible prophecy that
is issued twice monthly.

Rapture Ready Ministry — Todd Strandberg
1011 W. 31 Ave., Bellevue, NE 68005
phone: (402) 292-6167
email: todd@raptureready.com
website: www.raptureready.com
   An Internet ministry that provides a rich variety of Bible
prophecy study materials and links to other prophetic ministries. Keeps a unique, updated "Rapture Index" that analyzes
the intensity of prophetic developments in the world.

Revelation Illustrated — Pat Marvenko Smith
1740 Ridgeview Dr., North Huntingdon, PA 15642
phone: 1-800/327-7330
email: revill@aol.com
website: www.revelationillustrated.com
   Provides a magnificent series of illustrations of scenes
throughout the Book of Revelation. The illustrations are available in slides, prints, posters, and overhead transparencies. A
CD containing all the illustrations has been produced for
PowerPoint presentations.

Sounds of the Trumpet Ministries — Richard Booker
4747 Research Forest Dr., The Woodlands, TX 77380
phone: 281/469-1045
email: shofarprb@aol.com
website: www.booker.com

Conducts prophetic conferences, publishes books, and offers correspondence courses and tours to Israel. Runs an institute that teaches the Jewish roots of Christianity.

Southwest Radio Church — Noah Hutchings
P.O. Box 100, Bethany, OK 73008
phone: (405) 789-1222
email: info@swrc.com
website: www.swrc.com

Produces a nationally broadcast radio program and a monthly newsletter. Provides a great variety of books, tapes, and videos.

The Berean Call — Dave Hunt
P.O. Box 7019, Bend, OR 97708
phone: (541) 382-6210
email: from website
website: www.thebereancall.org

Provides extensive publishing on prophetic subjects. Produces an excellent monthly newsletter.

Thy Kingdom Come Ministry — Charles Pack
7301 E. 14th St., Tulsa, OK 74112
phone: (918) 835-6978
email: tkc@prophecywatch.com
website: www.thykingdomcometulsa.com

Produces a major prophecy conference each year and provides a bi-monthly prophetic newspaper. Also produces a bi-weekly webcast of audio programs at www.prophecywatch.com.

To His Glory Ministries — Vince Aquilino
P.O. Box 15031, Syracuse, NY 13215
phone: unlisted
email: vince@aplus-software.com
website: www.aplus-software.com/thglory
    Publishes a bi-monthly prophetic newsletter called *Prophecy and Current Events.*

World of the Bible Ministries — Randall Price
110 Easy Street, San Marcos, TX 78666
phone: 512/396-3799
email: wbmrandl@itouch.net
website: www.worldofthebible.com
    Produces books, videos, and tapes concerning biblical archeology and its relationship to Bible prophecy.

World Prophetic Ministry — Dave Breese
P.O. Box 907, Colton, CA 92324
phone: (909) 825-2767
email: from the website
website: www.thekingiscoming.com
    Sponsors a nationally televised program called "The King is Coming." Publishes a monthly prophetic newsletter.

Zola Levitt Ministries — Zola Levitt
P.O. Box 12268, Dallas, TX 75225
phone: (972) 690-1874
email: staff@levitt.com
website: www.levitt.com
    National television ministry featuring programs taped in Israel. Provides books, music, videos, and tours to Israel. Operates an Institute of Jewish-Christian Studies which offers correspondence courses.

About the Author

Dr. David R. Reagan is the evangelist for Lamb & Lion Ministries, a Bible prophecy ministry located in the Dallas, Texas, area.

Before founding the ministry in 1980, Dr. Reagan served for 20 years as a university professor, teaching international law and politics. Throughout that time he was an ardent student of the Bible.

Since 1980 Dr. Reagan has taught Bible prophecy in meetings and seminars held all across America and around the world. His daily radio program, "Christ in Prophecy," is broadcast throughout the United States. He has made many trips to Israel and is considered an expert on Middle East politics and Israel in Bible prophecy.

Dr. Reagan has been gifted with the skill to communicate complex ideas in simple, understandable terms. He is the author of several books, including the only children's book ever published about end-time Bible prophecy. It is entitled *Jesus Is Coming Again!* (Harvest House, 1992). His comprehensive book about Bible prophecy, entitled *The Master Plan* (Harvest House, 1993), has gone through many printings and has been published in many foreign languages. His most recent book is entitled *Living for Christ in the End Times* (Green Forest, AR: New Leaf Press, 2000).

Dr. Reagan and his wife, Ann, live in a Dallas suburb. They are the parents of two daughters, and have four grandchildren.

For a catalog of Dr. Reagan's tapes and publications, write to Lamb & Lion Ministries, P.O. Box 919, McKinney, TX 75070. You may also contact the ministry by telephone at (972) 736-3567 or by email at lamblion@lamblion.com. The ministry's website is located at www.lamblion. com.